With the Zionists in Gallipoli

by

John Henry Patterson

The Echo Library 2014

Published by

The Echo Library

Echo Library
Unit 22
Horcott Industrial Estate
Horcott Road
Fairford
Glos. GL7 4BX

www.echo-library.com

Please report serious faults in the text to complaints@echo-library.com

ISBN 978-1-40684-493-1

WITH THE ZIONISTS IN GALLIPOLI

BY

LIEUT. COL. J. H. PATTERSON, D.S.O.

AUTHOR OF "THE MAN-EATERS OF TSAVO,"
"IN THE GRIP OF THE NYIKA," ETC.

NEW YORK
GEORGE H. DORAN COMPANY

4

PREFACE

The narrative of the Zionists in Gallipoli has been written during the enforced idleness of the past month—a month which has been spent in endeavouring to recover sufficient health and strength to enable me to take a further, and, I trust, a more useful, hand in the Great Drama now approaching its climax.

In the following pages I have "set down nought in malice," neither have I given a word of praise where praise is not due—and more than due. My relations with those with whom I came into contact were excellent, and on the very rare occasions when they were otherwise, it was not due to any seeking of mine, but, unfortunately, my temperament is not such that I can suffer fools gladly.

My story is one of actual happenings, told just as I saw them with some suggestions thrown in, and if from these a hint is taken here and there by those in the "Seats of the Mighty," then so much the better for our Cause.

My chief object in writing this book is to interest the Hebrew nation in the fortunes of the Zionists and show them of what their Russian brothers are capable, even under the command of an alien in race and religion. Those who have the patience to follow me through these pages will, of course, see that I am not by any means an alien in sympathy and admiration for the people who have given to the world some of its greatest men, not to mention The Man who has so profoundly changed the world's outlook.

LONDON, 1916.

CONTENTS

6

WITH THE ZIONISTS IN GALLIPOLI

CHAPTER I. INTRODUCTION

I propose in the following pages to have something to say on the general policy of the Gallipoli campaign, and also upon the operations of war in execution of that policy. Now, in the discussion of these questions, I shall have some criticisms to make, so it may not be altogether inappropriate to give the reader some little idea of a few at least of my qualifications for such a rôle; otherwise he might well be tempted to say: "A fig for this fellow and his criticisms. What is he but a mere muleteer?"

Perhaps I may remark, to begin with, that when I took over the command of the Zion Mule Corps, I knew a great deal about soldiering and the art of war, but very little about the muleteer or the artful mule. But that's just "a way we have in the Army!"

From my boyhood I have either been a soldier or taken the keenest interest in soldiering, not only in England but in all parts of the world. My military experiences extend through home, India and South Africa, and have been by no means of a sketchy character. I spent the best part of three years in South Africa, where I commanded a Yeomanry regiment, and at times Regular troops of all arms, during the Boer War.

Those were glorious days—days when one could thoroughly enjoy warfare—a wild gallop over the veldt, a good fight in the open, and the day won by the best men.

In these days war is robbed of all its glory and romance. It is now but a dyke-maker's job, and a dirty one at that; but much as the soldier may dislike this method of warfare, it has come to stay, and we must make the best of a bad job, adapt ourselves to the new conditions, and by sticking it out, as we have always done, wear down the foe.

In addition to practical experience of soldiers and soldiering in England, India, and South Africa, I have watched our troops at work and play in many out-of-the-way parts of the Empire—the King's African Rifles in East Africa and Uganda; the Cape Mounted Rifles in South Africa; the "Waffs" in West Africa; the "Gippies" in Egypt, and the North-West mounted men of Canada away in the wilds of the Klondyke.

Nor have I confined my attention to the Empire's soldiers only.

In my various visits to America, I looked very keenly into the training and organisation of the American Army. I was especially fortunate in being able to do this, as I had the privilege of being Colonel Theodore Roosevelt's guest at the White House, while he was President, and his letters of introduction made me a welcome visitor everywhere. I saw something of the Cavalry and Artillery both East and West. I watched their Infantry amidst the snows of Alaska. I also noted what excellent game preservers the Cavalry troopers made in the Yellowstone Park—that wonderful

National Reserve, crammed with nature's wonders and denizens of the wild, where a half-tamed bear gave me the run of my life!

Whenever I was with American soldiers, their methods were so like our own that I never could feel I was with strangers.

There is only one fault to find with America's Army, and that is that there is not enough of it; for its size, I should say that it is one of the finest in the world. Never have I seen more efficiency anywhere, more keenness among officers and N. C. O.'s; and certainly never in any army have I eaten such delicious food as is supplied to the American private soldier; the soldiers' bread, such as I tasted at Fort Riley, baked in military ovens, cannot be surpassed at the "Ritz," "Savoy" or "Plaza."

It is incomprehensible to me why the average American should have such a strong prejudice against the Army. He seems to imagine that it is some vague kind of monster which, if he does not do everything in his power to strangle and chain up, will one day turn and rend him, and take all his liberties away.

To give some little idea of the feeling of Americans towards soldiers or soldiering, I will relate a little conversation which I overheard at Davenport, a town away out in the State of Iowa. I had had a very strenuous morning in the hot sun, watching the 7th Cavalry at squadron training and other work, and had got back to the hotel, thoroughly tired out after my arduous day. In the afternoon I was sitting on the shady side of the hotel which was on the main street; at a table near me were seated three Americans whose remarks I could not help overhearing; they were travellers in various small articles, one of them being a specialist in neckties; while they were talking two men of the 7th Cavalry walked past; my friend, the necktie man, looked after them, shook his head, and in most contemptuous tones said: "I suppose we must pay the lazy, useless brutes just for the look of the thing." The speaker was a pasty-faced, greasy, fat hybrid, about twenty-eight years old. I am afraid he was a type of which there are many in America; their God is the almighty dollar, an idol the blind worship of which will one day surely bring its own punishment.

Of course I do not, for a moment, wish it to be thought that people of this type predominate in America. I am happy to state that among her citizens I have met some of the most charming, hospitable, intellectual, unselfish and noble people to be found on the face of the globe.

America holds many interests for me, and I never fail to pay our cousins a visit when the opportunity occurs. Perhaps the chief of her attractions, so far as I am concerned, centre in and around the State of Virginia, that beautiful piece of country where most of the great battles of the Civil War were fought.

All my life I have made a point of studying military history and the campaigns of the great Captains of the past. Indeed, I have tramped over many battlefields in Europe, Asia, Africa and America, not at all with the idea that the knowledge would ever prove of value from a military point of view, but solely because I was deeply interested in soldierly matters.

In Spain and Flanders I have followed the footsteps of both Napoleon and Wellington.

In Canada I have sailed up the stately St. Lawrence, and with Wolfe in imagination again stormed the Heights of Abraham. When I stood on those heights some one hundred and fifty years after the great victory which added Canada to the Empire, I was able to realise, more fully than I had ever been able to do from books, the magnitude of the task which General Wolfe had before him when, on that fateful night of the 13th September, 1759, he led his troops up that precipitous road to victory.

In the United States I have, on horseback and on foot, followed Stonewall Jackson up and down the Shenandoah Valley, from Harper's Ferry (over the Potomac) to the Wilderness, where he was seized with such strange inertia, and on to that fatal Chancellorsville where an unlucky bullet, fired from his own lines, put an end to his life and all chances of victory for the South.

When I was at Washington, General Wotherspoon, the Chief of the War College there, very kindly supplied me with maps and notes which he had himself made of the battlefield of Gettysburg, and I am convinced that, if General Longstreet had arrived on the field in time, victory would have rested with the South; and I am equally convinced that, if Stonewall Jackson had been alive, Longstreet would have been in his proper place at the right time.

What a pity we have no Stonewall Jackson with us in these days. How noble is the epitaph on the monument of this great soldier. I only quote the words from memory, but they are something like this:

"When the Almighty in His Omnipotence saw fit to give victory
to the North over the South, He found that it was first necessary
to take to Himself Stonewall Jackson."

It was a great pleasure to me to see his wife, Mrs. Stonewall Jackson, when I was at Washington, but unfortunately I did not have the chance of speaking to her.

I was delighted to meet Miss Mary Lee several times, the daughter of the best loved General that ever led an Army—Robert E. Lee, the Commander-in-Chief of the Confederate Forces. Miss Lee gave me much pleasure by recounting many anecdotes about her famous father. Among other interesting reminiscences she told me that when the war broke out her youngest brother was a mere boy still at school, but the stirring accounts of the great fights in which his father commanded and his older brothers took part, so fired his ardour that one day he disappeared from school, and was not heard of by any of his family for the best part of a year. During this time he served as a soldier in a battery of Artillery. One day, while a furious battle was raging and the fortunes of war swayed first to the South and then to the North, General Lee observed some of his guns rapidly retiring from a particularly hot position. He galloped up to them himself and ordered them back into the fight. The Commander-in-Chief was somewhat surprised when a powder-blackened, mud-grimed young soldier, in a blood-stained shirt, said to him: "What, Dad, back into that hell again?"—and back into that hell the General sternly sent them at a gallop, and by so doing won the day for the South. Luckily, his boy came out of the battle unscathed and is alive to this day.

A few years ago I received an invitation from the German General Staff to visit Berlin. What I saw then, and on subsequent visits, impressed me very much with the thoroughness of the German nation, not only from a military, but also from a civil point of view.

A captain on the Staff was detailed to be my "bear-leader," while I was in Berlin. As we were strolling down Unter den Linden one day, discussing the youthfulness of senior officers of the British Army, as compared with those of the German Army, he confided to me that when he was ordered to conduct an English Colonel, he fully expected to see an old and grizzled veteran, whereas to his astonishment, he found me younger than himself, who was only a Captain. I shall never forget how, when I laughingly told him that I had jumped from Lieutenant to Lieutenant Colonel in about eight months during the South African War, he stopped short in the middle of the pavement, saluted me gravely and said: "You are Napoleon!" Of course, in these days, this meteoric flight is quite an everyday occurrence in our Army!

Among many other interesting things that the Prussian Captain showed me was their Hall of Glory, the walls of which are covered with pictures of famous battles and generals. While we were there I saw little parties of Prussian recruits being taken from picture to picture, guided by veterans. With straightened shoulders and glowing eye the old soldiers kindled the enthusiasm of the coming warriors by recounting to them the glorious and daring deeds performed by their forefathers on many a well-fought field.

This, no doubt, is only one of the numerous carefully thought out schemes of the General Staff to instil into the German nation the spirit of military pride and glory.

I paid another visit to Germany shortly before the present war broke out, and, soon after my return, I happened to meet in London the German Military Attaché, Major Renner, who seemed most anxious to hear from me what my impressions were. I suppose he wondered if I had seen much of the vast preparations, which were even then being made, for the great war into which Germany has plunged the world. Of all my observations the only things I confided to him (which he noted down as if they were of great importance!) were that I considered the abominable type used in German newspapers and books responsible for the be-spectacled German; that although their railway stations were wonderfully clean, yet they were without a decent platform, and my insular modesty had been shocked on many occasions by the amount of German leg I saw when the ladies clambered into and out of the carriages; and lastly, that I thought the long and handsome cloak worn by the officers might be greatly improved by making a slit at the side, so that the hilt of the sword might be outside, instead of inside the cloak, where not only did it make an unsightly lump, but was hard to get at in case of urgent need.

A day or two after war was declared, I happened to be dining in London with Mr. and Mrs. Walrond. Among the other guests was a Staff Officer from the War Office, Major R., who is now a general. Hearing that I had been recently in Germany, he asked me what I thought of their chances. I told him that I felt sure that Germany would have tremendous victories to begin with, and that I believed her armies would get to the gates of Paris, but did not think they would capture Paris this time; and that, although it would take us time, we would beat them eventually, for so long as we held command of the sea, we were bound to win in the end.

Some of the guests at this dinner party have since complimented me on the accuracy of the first part of my prophecy, and I feel absolutely convinced that the remainder of my forecast will, in spite of all bungling, prove equally true, always provided the Navy is given a free hand, and allowed to do its work in its own way.

In poor, brave little Belgium also I had every opportunity given to me by the General Staff to see their Cavalry at work; and while I was in Brussels, Colonel Fourcault, commanding the 2nd Guides, gave me the freedom of the barracks, where I could come and go as I liked. I became very good friends with the officers of the regiment, and we had discussions about Cavalry, its equipment and fighting value. On being asked for my opinion on the relative value of the rifle as compared with the lance and sabre, I unhesitatingly backed the rifle. I saw that the Belgian Cavalry were armed with a small, toylike carbine and a heavy sabre, and in the discussions which we had, I told them that in my humble opinion they would be well advised to scrap both and adopt the infantry rifle and a lighter thrusting sword—but above all I impressed upon them to be sure about the rifle, as the occasions for the use of the *arme blanche* in future would be rare, with all due deference to General von Bernhardi.

I was, of course, looked upon as a Cavalry leper for expressing such heretical opinions in a Cavalry mess, but I had my revenge later on, when Captain Donnay de Casteau of the 2nd Guides called on me at my club during his stay in London after poor little Belgium had been crushed. He came especially to tell me that those who were left of the regiment often talked of the unorthodox views I had so strongly expressed and he said: "We all had to agree that every word you told us has proved absolutely true."

While I was in Belgium I went down to the now famous Mons, and was the guest of the 7th Chasseurs à Cheval, where I got a thorough insight into the interior economy of the regiment.

It has always been a profound mystery to me that our Intelligence did not give Field-Marshal French earlier information while he was at Mons of the fact that large German forces were marching upon him from the direction of Tournai. Some strange and fatal inertia must have fallen both on the French Intelligence and our own, otherwise it would have been impossible for a large German army to have got into this threatening position without information having been sent to the Commander-in-Chief.

When in Spain I was privileged, owing to the courtesy of the Madrid War Office, to see something of the Spanish Army. I cannot say that I was deeply impressed; there was too much "*Mañana*" about it, or in other words, "Wait and see!" From what I observed I was not at all surprised to find it crumple up before the Americans in Cuba. It would, however, be a glorious thing to be a colonel in the Spanish Army, as they seemed to be able to do what was right in their own eyes.

But this was some years ago, and I understand that the Spanish Army, now that it has got a brand-new General Staff, is to be completely reorganised and made into a really efficient fighting force.

Of course I have many times seen the French and Italian armies at work and play—so that altogether my knowledge of soldiers and soldiering is somewhat catholic, and I may therefore claim to have some little right to criticise the policy, the strategy, and the tactics of the Gallipoli campaign.

CHAPTER II. GENERAL POLICY OF THE DARDANELLES CAMPAIGN

Many leaders of thought in England, whose convictions should certainly carry weight, are of the opinion that the expedition to the Dardanelles was in itself unsound, and should never have been undertaken. Now the views of well-known practical common-sense men should not be lightly thrust aside, but perhaps as one who has travelled and read much, and knows the East and the questions bound up with it fairly well, I hope I may not appear too presumptuous if I venture to disagree with those who condemn the Dardanelles policy.

It must be remembered that although we declared war on Turkey she had already committed several hostile acts on our Russian ally, and had flouted us most outrageously by allowing the *Goeben* and *Breslau* the freedom and protection of her waters and the resources of her arsenals.

Of course the escape of these two ships is one of the most extraordinary bungles of the war, which it is to be hoped will be carefully gone into at some future time, and the responsible culprit brought to book, for on his head probably rests the blood of the countless dead in Gallipoli.

I have reason to think that it is more than doubtful whether the mischievous activity of Enver Pasha and his satellites would have been sufficient to induce the Turkish nation to commit an act of war against either ourselves or Russia, but for the presence at the gates of Constantinople of these powerful German warships.

Our ally having been attacked and we ourselves flouted it became necessary for us, if we meant to uphold our prestige in the East, to declare war on Turkey.

A successful war against the Ottoman Empire had immense possibilities in it; the way to Russia would be opened, guns and munitions would have streamed in to her through the Bosphorus, while wheat for ourselves and our allies would have streamed out—but there was a great deal more than this at stake, as I shall point out.

It was well known to the Foreign Office that unless we showed a strong hand in the Near East, some of the Balkan States, who were even then trembling in the balance, would in all probability link their fortunes with those of the enemy. These wavering States wished to join the Allies if they saw a reasonable chance of the Allies' success. On the other hand Austria, backed up by the might of Germany, was at their gates, and with Belgium as an object lesson they feared for their country. What therefore could have been more calculated to gain them to our side than a smashing blow which would crumple up Turkey and give us direct communication with Russia? Had we succeeded (and we ought to have succeeded) it is certain that Greece and Rumania would now be fighting on our side; the astute Ferdinand would have seen on which side his bread was buttered, and have either kept Bulgaria neutral, or made common cause with the Allies; and those unfortunate little States, Serbia and Montenegro, would not have been betrayed and ground to dust.

The fall of Constantinople would once more have been a great epoch-making event, which would have changed the course of the world's history, for with its fall our victorious army, hand in hand with Russia, would have made a triumphant march through the Balkans, where every State would then have rallied to our side.

This allied flood would number between two and three millions of men, and with this irresistible force we would have burst upon the plains of Hungary and on to the heart of the Empire. Such an advance is not new to history, as the Turks themselves, when in the zenith of their power, overran Austria-Hungary and were only denied the domination of Europe under the very walls of Vienna itself, where, as everybody knows, they were defeated by John Sobiesky. No modern Sobiesky would have been found strong enough to deprive us of our prey, and with the fall of Vienna Austria would have been crushed, and the war would soon have come to a victorious end.

Even if we did not penetrate quite so far, the very fact of such a large army advancing from the south and east would have drawn an immense number of the enemy's troops from the Eastern and Western fronts, which would have given the Russians, the French and ourselves an opportunity of smashing through on those fronts and between us crushing Germany.

Yes, undoubtedly the fall of Constantinople was of vital importance, and for once our politicians were right.

In addition to our material gains in Europe, our prestige throughout the East would have reached a pinnacle such as it has never yet attained, and there would have been no such nuts for us to crack as the Egyptian, Persian, or Mesopotamian questions.

Germany would be completely hemmed in and the strangling grip of our fleet would have been irresistible when this last link with the outer world had been severed.

Germany's wheat supply from Rumania, copper from Serbia, cottons, fats and other vital products from Turkey would be cut off, and economic life in the Central Empires would in a very short time have been made intolerable.

CHAPTER III. STRATEGY AND TACTICS OF THE DARDANELLES CAMPAIGN

Now, having recognised the tremendous issues which were involved in the fall of Constantinople, it may be asked did the Government provide a weapon sufficiently strong to carry out their policy? In my humble opinion they did,—if only the weapon had been rightly handled.

Of course, whoever is to blame for the Bedlamite policy of the first disastrous attempts by the Navy alone bears a heavy responsibility. Beyond knocking the entrance forts to pieces, all that this premature attack by the Fleet effected was to give the Turks ample warning of our intentions, of which they took full advantage by making the Gallipoli Peninsula an almost impregnable fortress and the Dardanelles a network of mines.

But even this grave initial blunder could have been rectified, if only sound strategy had been adopted in the combined naval and military attack on the Dardanelles.

The problem before the strategists was, of course, to get through to Constantinople with the Fleet, and this could only be done by forcing the Narrows, a strip of the Dardanelles heavily fortified and only a mile wide. It was therefore necessary to reduce the forts guarding the Narrows, and with an army to hold the heights on Gallipoli dominating the Dardanelles, so as to ensure the safety of the Fleet.

Having command of the seas gave us the choice of launching the attack at any point we chose on the Turkish coast; therefore the Turks were at the great disadvantage of having to divide their forces into several parts, so as to guard such points as they thought might possibly be attacked.

It was known that there was a Turkish army on the Asiatic side, at the south of Chanak, the principal Fort on the Asiatic shore of the Narrows; also that the Bulair lines, some forty miles from the extremity of the Peninsula, were strongly fortified and held; that a strong force was entrenched on the southern portion of the Peninsula in the neighbourhood of Cape Helles; and, in addition, that there was yet another Turkish army holding the heights on the Ægean at, or near, a point now known as Anzac.

Now, if any one will take the trouble to study the map, which will be found at the end of this book, he will see that the key to the Narrows is that portion of the Gallipoli Peninsula which extends across from Anzac on the Ægean, through the heights of Sari Bair, to the Dardanelles.

If, therefore, instead of dividing the Mediterranean Expeditionary Force (which unfortunately was the plan adopted) and having it held up or destroyed in detail, the whole force had been thrown in its entirety at this point, and a vigorous sledge-hammer blow delivered, I feel absolutely confident that a crowning victory would have been gained and the expedition would have been a glorious success.

Of the four Turkish armies the only one that could have opposed a sudden vigorous thrust at the key position was the one at and near Anzac, and this force we could have swept aside and crumpled up before any of the others could possibly have come to its assistance.

That the Expeditionary Force could have been landed here is proved by the fact that the two Australian and New Zealand Divisions did land here, and these dauntless men, by themselves, almost succeeded in taking Sari Bair and getting astride the Peninsula. For eight months they held their end up, and more than held it up, against overwhelming odds. Had they been backed up at the time of the first landing on April 25th, 1915, by the "incomparable 29th Division," one of the best the British Army has ever seen, together with the two French Divisions, with their hundred celebrated .75 guns, and the Royal Naval Division, no Turkish troops at that time in the neighbourhood could for a moment have stood up against them, and with our grip once established on the Peninsula nothing could have shaken us off—not all the soldiers in the Ottoman Empire.

Every Turk on the southern portion of Gallipoli must inevitably have fallen into our hands within a few days, for it was well known that they were but ill supplied with ammunition and food. There was no chance of escape for them, for our Fleet commanded all the waters round Gallipoli up to the very Narrows themselves, and nothing could possibly have gained the Asiatic shore; while anything attempting to cross at the Narrows would have been inevitably sunk by the artillery which we would have mounted on the dominating heights of the Peninsula. No help could reach them from Constantinople, for the same reason, and it would have been in vain for them to have endeavoured to break through our lines, as was proved over and over again in the many determined but futile assaults they made on us in Gallipoli, when they were invariably hurled back with enormous losses.

Once astride the Peninsula, where our length of front would be less than seven miles, with over six men to the yard holding it, nothing could have shaken off our strangling hold. It would only then have been a question of directing the fire of the heavy naval guns on the Forts in the Narrows, which would, of course, be done by direct observation, and these strongholds would have been pounded to dust by the *Queen Elizabeth* and other battleships within a week, thus leaving open the road to Constantinople. Such might have been the glorious ending of the Gallipoli campaign if only sound strategical and tactical methods had been employed.

It is a thousand pities that this plan of operations was not adopted, for with such proved commanders as General d'Amade, General Birdwood and General Hunter-Weston—thrusters all—and with such incomparable men, there would have been no "fatal inertia" to chronicle.

It must be remembered that at the time of this landing on April 25th, the Turks had had but little time to organise their defences and it would then have been a much easier task to have seized the heights of Sari Bair than when the attempt was made with raw troops later on in August, an attempt which, even with all the drawbacks chronicled against it, came within an ace of being a success.

Another great advantage was that the weather, when we landed in April, was much cooler; there was also an ample rainfall, so that there would have been no difficulty about drinking-water, a lack of which in August proved fatal to the attempt made in that hot, dry month. We did not, of course, rely upon a chance rainfall at the time of our landing, for, as I shall show later on, ample provision had been made for carrying and supplying water, at all events for the 29th Division.

Unfortunately, such a plan of campaign as I have outlined was not put into execution. Instead, the force was split up into no less than nine parts, and practically destroyed in detail, or brought to a standstill by the Turks.

The Australian and New Zealand Divisions landed at Anzac, the key position; the 29th Division beat themselves to death attacking six different and almost impregnable positions on the toe of the Peninsula, where, I dare to say, not a single man ought ever to have been landed; in addition to the opposition they met with in Gallipoli they were subjected to a rain of shells from Asia, not only at the time of landing but throughout the whole time we wasted in occupying this utterly (from a military point of view) useless end of the Peninsula.

The Royal Naval Division was sent somewhere in the direction of the Bulair Lines, where it effected nothing, and the two French Divisions made an onslaught on the Asiatic coast, which, although well conceived and most gallantly put into execution, helped the main cause not at all. Of course, they were invaluable in preventing the Asiatic guns from firing on the 29th Division at the time of the landing, but then this Division should of course have been landed at Anzac, where they would have been out of range of those guns. Whatever Turkish force opposed the French at Kum Kale could never have got across the Dardanelles in time to have opposed our landing at or near Anzac.

If it had been thought necessary to make demonstrations on the Asiatic coast, at the toe of the Peninsula, and at the Bulair Lines, this could have been done equally well by sending the empty transports to those places, escorted by a few gunboats, and thus have held the Turks in position by making a pretence at throwing troops ashore at those points.

Of course, it is easy to be wise after the event, but I never did see, and never could see, the point of dividing our force and landing on the southern part of Gallipoli, for, once we had got astride the Peninsula from Anzac to the Narrows, all the Turks to the south of us must have fallen into our mouths, like ripe plums.

Napoleon has placed it on record that it is the besetting sin of British commanders to fritter away their forces by dividing them and so laying themselves open to be defeated in detail. It would appear that we have not even yet taken Napoleon's maxim to heart, for if ever there was an occasion on which it was absolutely vital to keep the whole force intact for a mighty blow, it was on that fateful Sunday morning, April 25th, 1915, when one concentrated thrust from Anzac to the

Narrows would have undoubtedly placed in our hands the key of the Ottoman Empire.

The Dardanelles campaign will go down to history as the greatest failure sustained by British arms, and yet no more glorious deeds have ever been performed by any army in the world.

CHAPTER IV. FORMATION OF THE ZION MULE CORPS

From the days of my youth I have always been a keen student of the Jewish people, their history, laws and customs. Even as a boy I spent the greater part of my leisure hours poring over the Bible, especially that portion of the Old Testament which chronicles battles, murders, and sudden deaths, little thinking that this Biblical knowledge would ever be of any practical value in after life.

It was strange, therefore, that I, so imbued with Jewish traditions, should have been drawn to the land where the Pharaohs had kept the Children of Israel in bondage for over four hundred years; and it was still more strange that I should have arrived in Egypt just at the psychological moment when General Sir John Maxwell, the Commander-in-Chief, was looking out for a suitable officer to raise and command a Jewish unit.

Now, such a thing as a Jewish unit had been unknown in the annals of the world for some two thousand years—since the days of the Maccabees, those heroic Sons of Israel who fought so valiantly, and for a time so successfully, to wrest Jerusalem from the grasp of the Roman legions.

It had happened that there had come down to Egypt out of Palestine many hundreds of people who had fled from thence to escape the wrath of the Turks. These people were of Russian nationality but of Jewish faith, and many of them strongly desired to band themselves together into a fighting host and place their lives at the disposal of England, whom the Jews have recognised as their friend and protector from time immemorial. Indeed, by many it is held that the British people are none other than some of the lost tribes; moreover, we have taken so much of Jewish national life for our own, mainly owing to our strong Biblical leanings, that the Jews can never feel while with us that they are among entire strangers.

Now these people having made known their wishes to the Commander-in-Chief, he, in a happy moment of inspiration, saw how much it would benefit England, morally and materially, to have bound up with our fortunes a Jewish fighting unit.

The next thing to be done was to find a suitable British officer to command this unique force, and at the time of my arrival in Cairo, General Maxwell had already applied for "a tactful thruster" to be chosen from among the officers of the Indian Brigade then doing duty on the Suez Canal.

My opportune arrival, however, coupled with a strong backing from an old friend, Major-General Sir Alexander Godley, decided him to offer me the command.

It certainly was curious that the General's choice should have fallen upon me, for, of course, he knew nothing of my knowledge of Jewish history, or of my sympathy for the Jewish race. When, as a boy, I eagerly devoured the records of the glorious deeds of Jewish military captains such as Joshua, Joab, Gideon and Judas Maccabæus, I little dreamt that one day I, myself, would, in a small way, be a captain of a host of the Children of Israel!

On the 19th March, 1915, I was appointed to my unique command, and on the same day I left Cairo for Alexandria, where all the refugees from Palestine were gathered together as the guests of the British Government.

On my arrival there, I lost no time in getting into touch with the leading members of the Jewish Community, and I found the Grand Rabbi (Professor Raphael della Pergola), Mr. Edgard Suares, Mr. Isaac Aghion, Mr. Piccioto and others, all most sympathetic and eager to assist me in every possible way. Nor must I forget that an impetus was given to the recruiting by the receipt of a heartening cablegram from Mr. Israel Zangwill, whose name is a household word to all Zionists.

On the 23rd March, 1915, the young Jewish volunteers were paraded for the purpose of being "sworn in" at the refugee camp at Gibbari.

It was a most imposing ceremony; the Grand Rabbi, who officiated, stood in a commanding position overlooking the long rows of serious and intelligent-looking lads. He explained to them the meaning of an oath, and the importance of keeping it, and impressed upon them that the honour of Israel rested in their hands. He then asked them to repeat after him, word for word, the oath of military obedience to myself and such officers as should be appointed over them, and with great solemnity, and in perfect unison, the men, with uplifted hands, repeated the formula.

The Grand Rabbi then delivered a stirring address to the new soldiers, in which he compared them to their forefathers who had been led out of Egypt by Moses, and at the end he turned to me and presented me to them as their modern leader.

This memorable and historic scene aroused the greatest enthusiasm among the throng of Jewish sympathisers who had come to witness this interesting ceremony.

The sanctioned strength of the Corps in officers and men was roughly 500, with 20 riding horses for officers and the senior non-commissioned officers, and 750 pack mules for transport work.

To assist me in commanding the Corps, I had five British and eight Jewish officers.

The Grand Rabbi of Alexandria, a most pious, earnest and learned man, was appointed our honorary chaplain.

I was extremely fortunate in my British officers, for although they had never served in the Army, or knew anything about military routine, yet they were all practical men, and, after all, at least in war-time, everything depends upon having officers with plenty of common sense.

I had Mr. D. Gye, who was lent to me from the Egyptian Ministry of Finance; Messrs. Carver and Maclaren, expert bankers and cotton-brokers; and the two brothers, Messrs. C. and I. Rolo, whose business house is known not only in Egypt, but also in the greater part of the world.

I was, indeed, lucky in getting such good men who loyally seconded me in everything and quickly mastered the details necessary for the running of the Corps;

nor did they spare themselves during those four weeks of slavery which we together put in while getting the men ready for active service.

In addition to these British officers, I had, as I have already stated, eight Jewish officers. One of these, Captain Trumpledor, had already been a soldier in the Russian Army, had been through the siege of Port Arthur, where he had lost his left arm, and had been given the Order of St. George (in gold) by the Czar for his gallantry and zeal during that celebrated siege.

Among the N. C. O.'s and men I had every conceivable trade and calling; highly educated men like Mr. Gorodisky, a Professor at the Lycée in Alexandria, and afterwards promoted to commissioned rank; students of Law, Medicine, and Divinity; mechanics of all kinds, of whom I found the tinsmith the most useful. Even a Rabbi was to be found in the ranks, who was able to administer consolation to the dying and burial rites to those who were struck down when death came amongst us before the enemy in Gallipoli. I also discovered among the enlisted soldiers a fully-qualified medical man, Dr. Levontin, whom I appointed our surgeon after having obtained permission to form a medical unit.

Through the kindness and practical sympathy of Surgeon-General Ford, the Director of Medical Services in Egypt, I soon had a hospital in being, with its tents, beds, orderlies and sanitary section.

Altogether we were a little family unit complete within ourselves.

I divided the Corps, for purposes of interior economy, into four troops, each with a British and Jewish officer in command; each troop was again divided into four sections with a sergeant in charge, and each section was again subdivided into subsections with a corporal in charge; and so the chain of responsibility went down to the lively mule himself—and, by the shades of Jehoshaphat, couldn't some of those mules kick!! Sons of Belial would be a very mild name for them.

One of the first things to be attended to was to find a suitable place upon which to train the men and mules. I eventually secured an excellent site at Wardian from Brigadier-General Stanton, then commanding at Alexandria. Here we pitched our tents and went into camp on April 2nd, 1915.

It was no light task to get uniforms, equipment, arms, ammunition, etc., for such a body of men at short notice, but in a very few days I had my men all under canvas, my horses and hundreds of mules pegged out in lines, and the men marching up and down, drilling to Hebrew words of command.

Never since the days of Judas Maccabæus had such sights and sounds been seen and heard in a military camp; indeed, had that redoubtable General paid us a surprise visit, he might have imagined himself with his own legions, because here he would have found a great camp with the tents of the Children of Israel pitched round about; he would have heard the Hebrew tongue spoken on all sides, and seen a little host of the Sons of Judah drilling to the same words of command that he himself used to those gallant soldiers who so nobly fought against Rome under his banner; he would even have heard the plaintive soul-stirring music of the Maccabæan hymn chanted by the men as they marched through the camp.

Although Hebrew was the language generally used, nevertheless I drilled the men in English also, as it was fitting that they should understand English words of command.

The men were armed with excellent rifles, bayonets and ammunition, all captured from the Turks when they made their futile assault on the Suez Canal.

For our badge we had the "Magin David," an exact reproduction of the Shield of David, such as he perhaps used when, as the Champion of Israel, he went out to fight Goliath of Gath.

It may, perhaps, be wondered why we were equipped with rifles, bayonets and ammunition, but this is one of the unique things about this unique Corps that, although it was only a Mule Corps, yet it was a fighting unit, and of this, of course, the men were all very proud.

When we were getting our equipment from Cairo, I left Lieutenant Carver there to draw it from the Arsenal in the Citadel and bring it to Alexandria, telling him that above all things he must never lose sight of the gear, for if he did it would certainly be appropriated by somebody else.

Among other things, he was drawing pack saddlery for our mules, which I was anxious to obtain quickly in order to go on with the training of the men.

Carver saw the pack saddles safely put into the railway wagons at Cairo, saw the wagons locked, sealed, and consigned to me at Alexandria, but the moment they arrived at Gibbari a prowling marauder from the Royal Naval Division, happening to spot the wagons and see what they contained by the ticket on the outside, induced the "Gippy" station-master to deliver them to him, and before I even knew that they had arrived at the station, all my pack saddles were safely on board ship and on their way to Suez with the Naval Division!

I tracked down the culprit, who not only had to disgorge but, I understand, to pay for the transit of the saddlery back to Alexandria; although this may have been a lesson for the buccaneer and might for the future make him "tread lightly" like Agag, yet it did not compensate me for the annoying delay caused by this unblushing robbery.

The work of training went on from dawn to dark, as officers and men had to be taught everything from the ground-floor up. Not a moment could be wasted. Drilling and parades were the order of the day; horses and mules had to be exercised, fed and watered three times a day; the men had to be taught how to saddle and unsaddle them, load and unload packs; they had also to be instructed in the use of the rifle and bayonet. Camp kitchens had to be constructed. Horse and mule lines had to be swept and garnished, tents cleaned out, etc., and a thousand and one things crammed into the day's work.

Notwithstanding the zeal and energy which we all put forth to get the Corps ready, yet had it not been for the sympathy of General Maxwell, and the active help of his Staff Officer, Captain Holdich, I fear it would have been impossible for us to have made the rapid progress we did in such a short space of time. I think it must be, in its way, a record to form, equip and train a unit of this description and have it actually in the firing line, and doing useful work there, in a little over three weeks!

It speaks volumes for the keenness of the men, and for the intelligent way in which they imbibed the knowledge which was crammed into them in such feverish haste.

After a couple of weeks' training we were specially favoured by a notification that the Commander-in-Chief of the Mediterranean Expeditionary Force, General Sir Ian Hamilton, would inspect us. It was with mixed feelings that I received this order, for, of course, it meant a special parade, and also that the whole of the routine of drills, etc., would have to be knocked out for one afternoon, and as every moment was precious this was no light matter.

The Commander-in-Chief came and made his inspection a few days before he sailed for Mudros, and was most complimentary on the workmanlike appearance which the Corps presented.

I was delighted to receive about this time a notification that my Corps should be held in readiness to embark for the front at an early date.

A few days before we embarked I had the privilege of partaking of the Feast of the Passover with the Grand Rabbi and his family at Alexandria. It will readily be understood with what feelings of deep interest I took part in the various rites. I seemed to be living again in the days of Moses when, in this very same land and not very far distant, the Children of Israel sprinkled their doorposts with the blood of the lamb, and partook of the Feast with their loins girded, their staves in their hands, on the eve of their departure from the land of bondage. I had to ask myself if it were all a dream. It seemed so strange that I should be partaking of the same Feast four thousand years later on the eve of my departure, with a number of the Children of Israel, to wander and suffer anew in another wilderness.

Every bit of the ceremony was gone through, the eating of unleavened bread and bitter herbs, the drinking of wine and vinegar, each symbolical of the trials to be gone through by the Israelites before reaching the Promised Land. All had its charm for me, and when my hostess came round with a towel and ewer and basin, to wash my hands at certain times during the Feast, it visualised to me as nothing else could have done those far away days when Pharaoh ruled the land.

The Grand Rabbi had his three handsome boys at his knees, the youngest a living image of one of Murillo's cherubs. He recounted to them in Hebrew the story of their forefathers' sojourn in Egypt, and their subsequent wanderings in the wilderness, as no doubt the same story has been told by the Fathers of Israel to their children for countless generations. "And thou shalt show thy son in that day, saying: This is done because of that which the Lord did unto me when I came forth from Egypt."

During our training period in Alexandria, we were the recipients of many acts of kindness from the community there. The men were given gifts by a committee of ladies, composed of the Baronne Felix de Menasce, Madame Rolo, Madame Israel, Mesdames E. and J. Goar, and a host of others.

We had a last big parade, and marched from Wardian Camp for some three miles through the streets of Alexandria to the Synagogue, to receive the final blessing of the Grand Rabbi. The spacious Temple, in the street of the Prophet Daniel, was on this occasion filled to its utmost capacity. The Grand Rabbi exhorted the men to bear themselves like good soldiers and in times of difficulty and danger to call upon the Name of the Lord who would deliver them out of their adversity. His final benediction was most solemn and impressive, and will never be forgotten by those who were privileged to be present.

A couple of days later we received orders to embark for Gallipoli with all possible speed. We therefore strained every nerve to get aboard in good time and in ship-shape order.

The Corps was divided into two parts, the Headquarters and two troops going on H. M. Transport *Hymettus*, and two troops on H. M. Transport *Anglo-Egyptian*.

It was no easy task in so short a time to get men, mules, horses, forage, equipment, etc., from Wardian Camp to the docks, a distance of two or three miles, and we worked practically all day and all night slinging horses and mules on board, tying them up in their stalls, and storing baggage and equipment, etc., in the holds. Thirty days' forage for the animals and rations for the men were also put under the hatches.

As one of our duties in Gallipoli would be to supply the troops in the trenches with water, an Alexandrian firm had been ordered to make some thousands of kerosene oil tins, the manufacture of which is a local industry. Wooden frames had also been ordered to fit on to the pack saddles, so as to enable the mules to carry the tins. Each mule was to carry four of these full of water, equal to sixteen gallons. The tins arrived in good time, but the wooden frames were late in delivery, and held us up over a day and a half beyond our time in Alexandria Docks.

At last, having obtained delivery of the indispensable wooden crates, we joyfully steamed out of harbour *en route* for Gallipoli on the 17th April, 1915.

CHAPTER V. ARRIVAL AT LEMNOS

We were not the only troops on board the *Hymettus.* There were some gunner officers of siege batteries, and some officers and men of the Royal Army Medical Corps; a stationary hospital with the necessary staff of the R. A. M. C. men, as well as some other odds and ends for various units of the Expeditionary Force already at Lemnos. I happened to be the Senior Officer on board, so was Officer Commanding the troops during the voyage.

I would like to mention here that the captain, chief officer, and chief engineer, of the *Hymettus* were most helpful in every possible way, and I am glad to be able to pay this little tribute to them for all their kindness to us while we were aboard.

One of the most interesting of our fellow voyagers was Captain Edmunds, R. A. M. C., one of the medical officers in charge of the Australian Hospital stores. He had been taken prisoner by the Germans while attending to the wounded during the retreat from Mons, and he told us many tales of his bad treatment at their hands. He was kept a prisoner for a considerable time, but finally was released owing to some interchange of medical officers between England and Germany.

The voyage to Lemnos was quite uneventful. We, fortunately, missed the Turkish torpedo-boat that tried to sink the *Manitou,* a transport just ahead of us. This troopship had quite an adventurous time. The torpedo-boat stopped her and the Turkish commander, with rare humanity, called out that he would give them ten minutes to save themselves. I am told that there was a German officer on the bridge who was heard quarrelling with the Turkish commander for being so lenient.

The *Manitou* lowered her boats in a very great hurry, and unluckily a couple of them tilted up, with the result that some fifty or sixty men were drowned. At the end of the time limit the Turks discharged a torpedo. Now when this missile is first fired it takes a dive before it steadies itself on its course, and as the two vessels were close together, luckily for the *Manitou,* the dive took the torpedo well under her keel; the same thing happened when the second and third torpedoes were launched; finally, as the Turk was about to open fire and sink the troopship with his guns, a British destroyer raced up at full speed and chased the marauder on to the rocks of a Grecian isle, where the Turkish vessel became a total wreck.

The training of the Zionists went steadily forward on board ship, for many of the men were still quite raw—in fact, I recruited several on the ship a few hours before we sailed. The mules and horses took up a great deal of time every day, but we never had one sick or sorry; and I may say here that we never lost one from sickness all the time we were in Gallipoli, which must, I think, be a record.

On April 20th we arrived at Lemnos and anchored just inside the entrance of Mudros harbour in a blinding wind and rain storm. It will be remembered that when the gods quarrelled, Jove hurled Vulcan out of Olympus on to Lemnos, where he established a forge underground. The morning following our arrival, one of the transports to windward of us began to drag her anchor, so our captain weighed immediately, fearing a collision, and we sailed right through the fleet to the opposite end of the great land-locked harbour. Never in all my life had I seen such a mighty armada of battleships, cruisers, destroyers, transports, etc. The *Queen Elizabeth* was there, looking for all the world like a floating fortress. There were some quaint French battleships, while the Russian cruiser *Askold* caused universal attention, owing to her five slim funnels. With the soldier's customary knack of giving appropriate names, the *Askold* was known throughout the Fleet as "the packet of Woodbines." Our Zionists, as we sailed by, astonished her crew by bandying words with them in Russian.

Our trip up the harbour was not to end without adventure, for, on turning round to cast anchor, our ship ran aground on a mudbank. Here we stuck fast and all the King's horses and all the King's men failed to tug us off again. Time after time naval officers came along with tug-boats and vessels of various kinds which strained to release us, but each attempt was a hopeless failure.

On the afternoon of the 23rd, I got somewhat of a shock on being informed that the Zion Mule Corps was to be divided. The half on the *Hymettus* was to go with the 29th Division, and the other half, those already on board the *Anglo-Egyptian*, were to be sent with the Australians and New Zealanders. Of course, this arrangement would have been all right if these three Divisions had been landed at the same place, but as they were to disembark some dozen miles apart it would be impossible for me to keep an eye on both halves of the Corps, and I greatly feared that the half away from my own personal supervision would not prove a success, for officers, N. C. O.'s and men were entirely new to soldiering, and it was too much to expect that they could go straight into the firing line, after only some three weeks' training, and come through the ordeal triumphantly without an experienced commander.

I, therefore, after many vain endeavours to get away, hailed a passing launch, which, as a great favour, put me on board the staff ship, the *Arcadian*, where I had an interview with the Deputy Quartermaster-General, and begged of him not to divide the Corps, as I feared that those away from my control would prove but a broken reed. He told me, however, that it was impossible to alter matters, and that the Australians and New Zealanders had had practically no transport, except what my Corps would supply, and that in any case we would not be separated for more than four days, because if we could not crush the Turks in that time, between the two forces, we were going to give up the attempt and return to our ships.

Well, we did not crush the Turks in the four days, and, having failed, it was not so easy to get away, and the result was that, owing to lack of experience, and mismanagement in the handling of them, the two troops with the Australians, after a couple of weeks' service with that force, were sent back to Alexandria, without any reference to me, and there disbanded.

As there were no boats available, I had the greatest difficulty in getting away from the *Arcadian*, and it was only after wasting many valuable hours and meeting with many rebuffs, that I eventually got a kind-hearted sailor to give me a lift back to the *Hymettus*. A few steam launches were badly needed to enable commanding officers to go aboard the staff ship to discuss with the chiefs of the various departments such items as can only be settled satisfactorily at a personal interview.

I must say that I was not at all pleased with our position on the mudbank, where, in spite of all efforts to move us, we still remained stuck. In the first place, I feared that we would be unable to get away with the rest of the transports on the morning of the 25th, the date fixed for the great attack, and even if by chance another vessel could be found for us, it would mean transhipping all the men, horses, mules, baggage, forage and equipment, which would be an immense labour in an open harbour like Mudros, where it is often blowing half a gale. It is no wonder that, as each attempt at hauling off the *Hymettus* failed, I grew more and more anxious as to our ultimate chance of getting away in time to see the start of the great fight in Gallipoli.

At last, on the 24th, the naval officers engaged on the work gave up all further attempts to haul us off, and reported the task as hopeless—at any rate until everything was removed from the ship. In the course of an hour I received a signal from the Deputy Quartermaster-General to tranship all my corps, stores, etc., from the *Hymettus* to the *Dundrennon*, a transport lying half a mile or more away. On receipt of this message I signalled back and asked for tugs and lighters to enable us to effect the transfer, but, although my signallers endeavoured for hours to attract the attention of those on the staff ship, I entirely failed to get any reply. I finally tried to extort a response of some sort by sending an ire-raising message to the effect that on investigation, I found that many of the men and mules could not swim! But my sarcasm was wasted, for the *Arcadian* remained dumb.

This failure in the signalling arrangements was very marked all through the two or three days we spent at Lemnos. It was practically impossible to get any message through, and one felt completely cut off from all communication with the staff ship. There were no arrangements for getting about in the harbour. The ship's small boats would have been swamped in the heavy sea, and it was practically impossible to secure a launch.

This failure, together with the wretched signalling arrangements, gave me serious qualms, and I could not help wondering if the muddle ceased here, or did it extend to other and more grave matters which would imperil the success of the expedition?

All day long I was anxiously on the look-out for a tug and lighters to enable me to tranship to the *Dundrennon*, and at last, at about 6 P.M., I saw a little trawler, towing a string of half a dozen lighters, making her way up the harbour towards us. In a few minutes they were alongside and made fast to the *Hymettus*, but, alas! I soon discovered that, although the lighters were for us, the tug was about to sail away again. The only order the commander had received was to bring the lighters alongside and make them fast to the *Hymettus*, and there his task ended. This was a blow to me, for I felt that, if the little *Jessie* went off, I and my Corps would be left high and dry on the Lemnos mud, while the rest of the Expedition sailed off next morning on the great adventure! Luckily, the commander of the *Jessie* was a friend of the Captain's and came on board for a yarn. After a few moments I followed him to the Captain's cabin and, on being introduced, found that he was Mr. A. R. Murley. I soon discovered that he was a most exceptional man in every way, and a sailor to his finger tips. He had been Chief Officer on board a large liner, but had resigned his post to volunteer his services to the Admiralty for the war, and, although the position he now held as skipper of the *Jessie* was a very small one compared with his last charge, yet, as he sportingly said, what did it matter so long as he was usefully doing his bit?—and I believe he was as proud of the *Jessie* as if she had been a liner or a battleship.

I used all my eloquence on Mr. Murley, pointed out what a desperate position I was in, and said that if he did not come to my aid we would, indeed, be hopelessly stranded. The Captain of the *Hymettus*, who, by the way, was naturally very much upset at having struck this uncharted mudbank, ably seconded my appeal, and although Murley had been working from dawn and had intended to return to his depot to lay in stores of coal, water and oil, to enable him to start with the expedition at five o'clock in the morning, he agreed to work for me throughout the night.

CHAPTER VI. A STRENUOUS NIGHT

Having once obtained Murley's consent I flew off and got officers and men told off in reliefs, some to work on the loading up of the lighters, others to go with the mules to the *Dundrennon* and remain there to ship and stow away each load as it came over during the night.

There were six lighters, and as soon as three were filled, Murley got the little *Jessie* hitched on and towed them off to the *Dundrennon*. It was a joy to watch the masterly way in which he handled his tug and manoeuvred the tow of lighters into the exact position where they were required alongside the *Dundrennon*. Never did I see an error of judgment made, and everything that Murley had to do went like clockwork. He had a clear and pleasant word of command, which rang out like a bell, and although he was "a hustler" his men never resented it; first of all, because they knew he was top-hole at his job and, secondly, because he was extraordinarily tactful. Tow after tow went back and forth throughout the night—three full lighters to the *Dundrennon* and three empty ones back to the *Hymettus*—and didn't we just hustle those mules into the boats, and didn't they kick and bite as they felt the slings go round them to hoist them aloft! It would have taken us too long had we only slung one mule at a time, so we hoisted them in couples! The comical sight the brace of mules presented, as they were whipped off their legs and swung up into the gloom, can well be imagined. They kicked and plunged as they were passed over the side and lowered down into the inky murkiness of the lighters, where they were caught and secured at much risk by men waiting there for the purpose. Heaven only knows how they escaped injury, for they had a very rough time of it before they were comfortably stowed away in their new quarters on the *Dundrennon*. I was quite prepared to hear of several casualties among both men and mules, but the mule is a hardy beast, and the Zionist can stand a lot of knocking about, and we had not a single man or animal injured.

We were exceptionally fortunate in finding on board the *Dundrennon* part of an Indian Mule Corps for service with the New Zealanders, commanded by Captain Alexander, and I cannot be sufficiently grateful to him for the way in which he set his men to work and helped us to put away and tie up our equipment and mules.

I cannot say so much for the help given me by the Captain of the *Dundrennon*, who was rather a rough customer, and curtly informed me that he had orders to sail at five o'clock A. M. sharp, and that, whether I was aboard or not, he meant to weigh anchor at that hour.

All night long we worked feverishly, slinging and unslinging with all possible haste, and while I was using everybody up to breaking point in my efforts to get through in time, Captain Edmunds, who was in charge of the medical stores for the Australians and New Zealanders, came up to me and told me of the hopeless plight in which he was placed. The Director of Medical Services had ordered him to get himself, his men and his stores as quickly as possible on board the *Anglo-Egyptian*, but here again no means were supplied to enable the order to be carried out. "I can hardly dare appeal to you," he continued, "to get me out of my difficulties, for I can see that you will hardly get your own lot transferred before five o'clock." I asked him if it was very necessary that he should be put aboard, and he told me that, so far as he knew, his were the only hospital stores available for the Australians and New Zealanders.

This was a very grave matter, and although I was very loth to give up all chance of completing the transfer of my own Corps within the time limit, yet I felt that this was a case which, at all hazards to my own fortunes, must be seen through, so that our gallant comrades from Australia and New Zealand might not lack the medical necessities which I knew would be required the moment they got into action.

I, therefore, turned my men on to loading up the hospital stores, and, when all was ready, Murley towed us across to the *Anglo-Egyptian*, where I eventually saw Captain Edmunds, his staff of R. A. M. C. men and his stores safely on board.

Some months afterwards Gye received a letter from Captain Edmunds, written from Anzac, in which he stated: "Remember me to Colonel Patterson and tell him from me that being able to get those stores on to the *Anglo-Egyptian* averted what would have been an appalling calamity from a medical point of view, as I do not know what this place would have done without my stores the first two days."

So I think that Australia and New Zealand owe me one for the help I gave them on that strenuous night of April 24th, when I was buried up to the neck in work of my own. It was a great strain on my feelings of duty to risk being left stuck on the mud, but I realised at the time that I was doing not only what was right, but what was essential from a military point of view; and when I read that letter from Edmunds, I felt very glad that I had risen to the occasion and had put the needs of the Australians and New Zealanders before my own.

By the time that the transfer was completed it was 3.30 A. M., and I then knew that I could not possibly get the remainder of my Zionists, mules, equipment and stores transferred to the *Dundrennon* by the time she was scheduled to sail. I, therefore, went to the Captain and laid my case before him, pointing out that it was impossible to get everything transferred in time and asking him would he delay sailing until we were aboard. I have said that he was rather a rough type of man. Having been for many years master of a tramp steamer, he had spent his life dealing with rough men and doing rough work. I have, therefore, no doubt that he thought he was answering me in quite a civil and polite way when he told me he would see me damned before he delayed his ship five minutes.

I then asked my good friend the skipper of the *Jessie* if he would run me down to the staff ship, as I hoped to be able to get a written order from somebody there, to the Captain of the *Dundrennon*, cancelling the sailing at 5 A. M. until such time as I would have my unit complete on board.

Off we sailed, threading our way in the dark through such of the few warships and transport vessels as had not yet sailed, and just before four o'clock I found myself knocking at the cabin door of a Naval Officer. After rapping for some time, he called out "Come in," but the door was locked, so he was obliged to get up to let me in, and

I am not surprised that his greeting to me was not exactly one of brotherly love. When I told him of my position and asked him to give me an order delaying the departure of the *Dundrennon*, he flatly refused to do it, and said that the hours of departure of the ships were fixed and that he was not the man to change the order: I would have to go to the Captain of H. M. S. *Hussar*, who was the man actually responsible for the sailings. I pointed out to him that by the time I reached the *Hussar*, which was still further off, and got at the Captain, and then made my way back to the *Dundrennon*, it would be long after five o'clock, and there would be no *Dundrennon* there, for the ship would have sailed! I urged that in a special case of this kind I hoped he would over-rule the Time-table. He was, however, most obdurate, and told me it was useless for me to argue with him any longer. When I pointed out to him that I had only received means of transferring my Corps late the previous evening, and that we had been working all through the night, he snapped at me and said, "Why do you make such a fuss about having worked all through the night? That is nothing." I quietly told him that I had once or twice in my life worked all night without making any fuss about it, and that I had merely wished to impress upon him that it was not through any fault or slackness on my part that the transfer could not be completed in time. He was not mollified, however, and practically marched me off to the gangway, where he turned about and made for his cabin. But I was not to be so easily shaken off, so I promptly turned about also and pursued him. I pointed out to him emphatically that, unless he gave me this order, on him would rest the entire responsibility of leaving the 29th Division in the lurch, as I remarked that my Corps was the only one to take them up food and water, and that if they died of thirst he would be entirely to blame. "What is the good of sending off the *Dundrennon*" I asked, "unless she has on board the Corps upon which so much depends? What will be said hereafter if you let the 29th Division die of thirst?"

This last appeal moved the naval man's bowels of compassion; so without more ado he had the office opened up, and wrote out an official order delaying the sailing of the *Dundrennon* until 8 o'clock. When I told him also that the master of the *Dundrennon* was not very helpful he at once wrote a curt note to him as follows:

"I hear that you are not aiding Colonel Patterson in his embarkation as much as you might. You had better do so."

I kept this note for emergency, in case the master of the *Dundrennon* might prove obstreperous, but I had no occasion to use it.

I was delighted with my success, and so was Murley, who was with me all the time I was endeavouring to persuade the naval man to order this very necessary delay. It was of course no light thing to take upon himself the responsibility of altering the Time-table. I can only say to him "Well done." We got back to the *Dundrennon* at a quarter to five and were greeted by the wrathful skipper, who was up and preparing his ship for a punctual start. I shouted up to him: "I have an order cancelling your sailing until eight o'clock. Do you want to see it?" "I do," was the gruff response. "Pass it up on this rope," throwing a line aboard the *Jessie*. I stuck the order between the strands of the rope and the skipper hauled it up, and as he read it he uttered highly flavoured maledictions on all naval and army men, without showing any undue partiality for either!

Now I was very glad that things had turned out so happily, but even if I had not obtained the order for the delay of the *Dundrennon*, I still had a trump card up my sleeve, which I had only intended to play in the last resort, namely, to have seized the anchor winch and, at all costs, have prevented any sailor from approaching it until I gave orders that they might do so. I had put fifty armed men on board ship, whom I was prepared to use for this purpose in case of necessity, as I was determined that I should go to Gallipoli complete, even at the risk of seizing the ship and being, later on, tried for piracy on the high seas!

This reminds me of an incident which happened in the South African War when I had to resort to almost similar methods. I was given orders to entrain my squadron instantly at Bloemfontein, but instead of being sent north we were merely shunted into the Station siding, where we had to remain for the best part of twenty-four hours without any chance of watering our horses. We started some time in the night, and at daybreak the train was halted at a siding where there was a stream running close by. I looked at my horses and found many of them down, owing to fatigue and want of water, so I ordered the men to unbox them and take them to water at the stream. When the guard saw this he strongly objected, saying that the train that was coming down might pass through at any moment, and that, as soon as it had passed, he would proceed on his way to Johannesburg, whether the horses were back in the boxes or not. I said: "Will you?" and he replied: "Yes, I will. I am in charge of this train and I am going to push on."

I thereupon called up the Sergeant-Major, whispered an order to him, and in two seconds that guard found himself a prisoner on the platform with a soldier on each side of him, with orders to hold him fast in case he made any attempt to get away. The watering was quietly and expeditiously proceeded with, and meanwhile the down train passed through.

Our engine driver came along the platform to see what was the matter and I overheard the guard telling him to proceed at once, even if he, the guard, were left behind. I asked the driver if he meant to carry out the guard's instructions and he replied: "Yes." I then said: "Sergeant-Major, two more men! make this driver a prisoner."

When the watering of the horses was over I released my prisoners and told them they could now go on. The driver refused. I said: "All right, then. I will drive myself." The look of astonishment that came over the driver's face when he saw me mount the footplate, confidently put my hand on the lever and start the train, was something to be remembered. He immediately caved in, jumped up and resumed his duties, without more ado. Some time afterwards I heard that the guard made a bitter complaint of my high-handedness, which eventually came before General Tucker, then commanding at

Bloemfontein, and it was a satisfaction to me to learn that the General emphasised his approval of what I had done in one of his choicest expressions.

Even with the extension of the time limit, I felt that it would be a close thing if we were to get everything on board the *Dundrennon* by eight o'clock, so we all worked with feverish energy, and it was only by a great spurt on the part of the *Jessie* that we finally got our last three lighters, loaded to their utmost capacity, made fast to the *Dundrennon* just before eight o'clock. I knew that it would still take a good hour to get everything aboard, so, drawing Murley aside, I suggested to him that he must be in need of a little refreshment after his strenuous night, and that if he were to go to the skipper's cabin he could, I felt sure, count on him to produce a bottle—and I added: "Make sure that he does not come out until I give you the signal."

Murley laughingly undertook this congenial task, and when, after everything had been stowed away, I eventually joined them at 9:10 A. M., I found the skipper thoroughly enjoying himself and laughing heartily at one of Murley's impromptu yarns. Bravo, Murley! If I am ever ruler of the "King's Navee"—and stranger things have happened—you may be sure that you will be appointed an Admiral of the Fleet!

I don't know how to find you, but if these lines ever come under your eye, remember that dinner that you are to have with me in London, and it shall be of the best, Murley, of the very best.

I found, after all, that the old skipper's bark was worse than his bite. He thawed towards me to such an extent that, when I parted from him at Gallipoli, he sped me on my way with a present of two precious bottles of his best whisky!—sign manual of his having taken me to his rugged but withal kindly old heart.

CHAPTER VII. DESCRIPTION OF SOUTHERN GALLIPOLI

As I shall have to mention several places in Gallipoli, it may be well before proceeding further to give the reader some idea of the geography of the place.

Gallipoli is a narrow, hilly peninsula, varying from three to twelve miles wide, running south-westward into the Ægean Sea, with the Dardanelles, from one to four miles wide, separating it from the Asiatic coast throughout its length of some forty miles.

As I am going to speak more particularly of the southern end of the Peninsula, I will only describe that portion of it, as it was here that the 29th Division landed, and the Zion Mule Corps worked.

The dominating feature is the hill of Achi Baba, some seven hundred feet high, which, with its shoulders sloping down on the one side to the Ægean and on the other to the Dardanelles, shuts out all further view of the Peninsula to the northward. There are only two villages in this area, Sedd-el-Bahr at the entrance to the Dardanelles, and Krithia, with its quaint windmills, to the southwest of Achi Baba, somewhat picturesquely situated on the slope of a spur, some five miles northwest of Sedd-el-Bahr—Achi Baba itself being between six and seven miles from Cape Helles, which is the most southerly point of the Peninsula.

A line through Achi Baba from the Ægean to the Dardanelles would be a little over five miles, while the width at Helles is only about one and a half miles.

A fairly good representation of this tract of country will be obtained by holding the right-hand palm upward and slightly hollowed, the thumb pressed a little over the forefinger. Imagine the Dardanelles running along by the little finger up the arm, and the Ægean Sea on the thumb side. Morto Bay, an inlet of the Dardanelles, would then be at about the tip of a short little finger; Sedd-el-Bahr Castle at the tip of the third finger; V Beach between the third finger and the middle finger; Cape Helles the tip of the middle finger; W Beach between the middle finger and the forefinger; X Beach at the base of the nail of the forefinger; Gully Beach between the tip of the thumb and the forefinger; Gully Ravine running up between the thumb and forefinger towards Krithia village, which is situated half-way up to the thumb socket; Y Beach at the first joint of the thumb; and Achi Baba in the centre of the heel of the hand where it joins the wrist.

Anzac, where the Australians and New Zealanders landed, would be some distance above the wrist on the thumb side of the forearm; and the Narrows of the Dardanelles would be on the inner or little finger side of the forearm opposite Anzac.

Imagine the sea itself lapping the lower part of the hand on a level with the finger-nails, and then the cliffs will be represented by the rise from the finger-nails to the balls of the fingers.

The hollowed hand gives a very good idea of the appearance of the country, which gradually slopes down to a valley represented by the palm of the hand. The lines on the hand represent the many ravines and watercourses which intersect the ground.

Practically the whole of this basin drains into Morto Bay or the Dardanelles, with the exception of Gully Ravine and the ravine running down to Y Beach, which drain into the Ægean Sea.

A glance at the "handy" sketch will make everything clear, but it does not pretend to strict accuracy.

CHAPTER VIII. A HOMERIC CONFLICT

Mudros Harbour was deserted as we sailed through it on our way out, for all the warships and transports had already left. Just beyond the harbour entrance we passed the *Anglo-Egyptian*, on the decks of which the other half of the Zionists were crowded. We wondered what had happened to detain her, for she was lying at anchor; but we saw nothing amiss, and lusty cheers were given and received as we steamed past.

When we had rounded the land which guards the entrance to the harbour, the *Dundrennon* turned her bows northeastward and we steamed off towards the land of our hopes and fears, through a calm sea, which sparkled gaily in the sunshine. The soft zephyr which followed us from the south, changed suddenly and came from the northeast, bringing with it the sound of battle from afar. The dull boom of the guns could now be plainly heard and told us that the great adventure had already begun. How we all wished that the *Dundrennon* were a greyhound of the seas and could rush us speedily to the scene of such epoch-making events! But, alas! she was only a slow old tramp, and going "all out" she could do no more than twelve knots an hour; and it seemed an eternity before we actually came close enough to see anything of the great drama which was being enacted.

As we ploughed along the calm sea, to the slow beat of the engines, each hour seemed a century, but at last we were able to distinguish the misty outline of the Asiatic shore and, a little later on, we saw, coming to meet us like an out-stretched arm and hand, a land fringed and half-hidden by the fire and smoke which enveloped it as if some great magician had summoned the powers of darkness to aid in its defence.

Soon battleships, cruisers and destroyers began to outline themselves, and every few minutes we could see them enveloped in a sheet of flame and smoke, as they poured their broadsides into the Turkish positions. The roar of the *Queen Elizabeth's* heavy guns dwarfed all other sounds, as this leviathan launched her huge projectiles— surely mightier thunderbolts than Jove ever hurled—against the foe. Every now and again one of her shells would strike and burst on the very crest of Achi Baba, which then, as it belched forth flame, smoke and great chunks of the hill itself, vividly recalled to my mind Vesuvius in a rage.

The whole scene was a sight for the gods, and those of us mortals who witnessed it and survived the day have forever stamped on our minds the most wonderful spectacle that the world has ever seen. Half the nations of the earth were gathered there in a titanic struggle. England, with her children from Australia and New Zealand, and fellow subjects from India; sons of France, with their fellow citizens from Algeria and Senegal; Russian sailors and Russian soldiers; Turks and Germans—all fighting within our vision, some in Europe and some in Asia.

Nor did the wonders end here, for, circling the heavens like soaring eagles, were French and British aeroplanes, while, under the sea, lurked the deadly submarine.

It was altogether in the fitness of things that this Homeric conflict should have its setting within sight of the classic Plains of Troy.

Who will be the modern Homer to immortalise the deeds done this day—deeds beside which those performed by Achilles, Hector and the other heroes of Greece and Troy pale into utter insignificance? Certainly a far greater feat of arms was enacted in Gallipoli on this 25th of April, 1915, than was ever performed by those ancient heroes on the Plains of Ilium, which lay calm, green and smiling just across the sparkling Hellespont.

Up the Dardanelles, as far as the Narrows, we could see our ships of war, principally destroyers, blazing away merrily and indiscriminately at the guns, both on the European and Asiatic shores. The sea was as calm as a mill-pond round Cape Helles—the most southerly point of the Peninsula; the only ripple to be seen was that made by the strong current shot out through the Straits. All round the men-of-war Turkish shells were dropping, sending up veritable waterspouts as they struck the sea, for, luckily, very few of them hit the ships. It was altogether the most imposing and awe-inspiring sight that I have ever seen or am likely to see again.

We were under orders to disembark, when our turn came, at V Beach, a little cove to the east of Cape Helles. As we approached near to our landing-place, we could see through the haze, smoke and dust, the gleam of bayonets, as men swayed and moved hither and thither in the course of the fight, while the roar of cannon and the rattle of the machine-guns and rifles were absolutely deafening. We could well imagine what a veritable hell our brave fellows who were attacking this formidable position must be facing, for, in addition to rifle and machine-gun fire from the surrounding cliffs, they were also at times under a deadly cannonade from the Turkish batteries established on the Asiatic shore.

The warships were slowly moving up and down the coast blazing away fiercely at the Turkish strongholds, battering such of them as were left into unrecognisable ruins.

We in the transports lay off the shore in four parallel lines, each successive line going forward methodically and disembarking the units on board as the ground was made good by the landing parties.

We watched the fight from our position in the line for the whole of that day, and never was excitement so intense and long-sustained as during those hours; nor was it lessened when night fell upon us, for the roll of battle still continued—made all the grander by the vivid flashes from the guns which, every few moments, shot forth great spurts of flame, brilliantly illuminating the inky darkness. Sedd-el-Bahr Castle and the village nestling behind it were fiercely ablaze, and cast a ruddy glare on the sky.

The next day, from a position much closer inshore, we watched again the terrible struggle of the landing-parties to obtain a grip on the coast. We were one and all feverish with anxiety to land and do something—no matter how little—to help the gallant fellows who were striving so heroically to drive the Turk from the strong positions which he had carefully fortified and strengthened in every possible way.

A most bloody battle was taking place, staged in a perfect natural amphitheatre, but never had Imperial Rome, even in the days of Nero himself, gazed upon such a corpse-strewn, blood-drenched arena.

This arena was formed partly by the sea, which has here taken a semicircular bite out of the rocky coast, and partly by a narrow strip of beach which extended back for about a dozen yards to a low rampart formed of sand, some three or four feet high, which ran round the bay. Behind this rampart the ground rose steeply upwards, in tier after tier of grassy slopes, to a height of about 100 feet, where it was crowned by some ruined Turkish barracks. On the right, this natural theatre was flanked by the old castle of Sedd-el-Bahr, whose battlements and towers were even then crumbling down from the effects of the recent bombardment by the Fleet. To the left of the arena, high cliffs rose sheer from the sea, crowned by a modern redoubt. Barbed wire zig-zagged and criss-crossed through arena and amphitheatre—and such barbed wire! It was twice as thick, strong and formidable as any I had ever seen.

The cliffs and galleries were trenched and full of riflemen, as were also the barracks, the ruined fort, and Sedd-el-Behr Castle. Machine-guns and pom-poms were everywhere, all ready to pour a withering fire on any one approaching or attempting to land on the beach.

It is small wonder, therefore, that so few escaped from that terrible arena of death. Indeed, the wonder is that any one survived that awful ordeal.

The little cove was peaceable enough on the morning of the 25th, when the Transport *River Clyde* steamed in. It was part of the scheme to run her ashore at this beach and, as it was known that the venture would be a desperate one, what was more fitting than that she should be filled with Irish soldiers (the Dublins and Munsters)—regiments with great fighting records? With them was also half a battalion of the Hampshire Regiment. Special preparations had been made to disembark the troops as quickly as possible. Great holes had been cut in the iron sides of the *River Clyde*, and from these gangways made of planking, which were of course lashed to the ship, sloped down in tiers to the water's edge. From the ends of these gangways a string of lighters stretched to the shore to enable the men to rush quickly to land.

In addition to those on the *River Clyde*, three companies of the Dublin Fusiliers were towed to the beach in open boats and barges by little steam pinnaces. It had been intended that these should steal in during the dark hours just before dawn, but, owing to miscalculations of the speed of the current, or some other cause, the boats did not arrive in time and only reached the shore at the same moment that Commander Unwin, R. N., of the *River Clyde*, according to the prearranged plan, coolly ran his vessel aground. This manoeuvre must have greatly astonished the Turks, but not a sound or move did they make, and it seemed at first as if the landing would not be opposed. As soon, however, as the Munsters began to pour from her sides, a perfect hail of lead opened on the unfortunate soldiers, who were shot down in scores as they raced down the gangway. Some who were struck in the leg stumbled and fell into the water, where, owing to the weight of their packs and ammunition, they went to the bottom and were drowned. For days afterwards these unfortunate men could be seen through the clear water, many of them still grasping their rifles.

The men in the boats suffered equally heavily and had even less chance of escape. Many were mown down by rifle fire and sometimes a shell cut a boat in two and the unfortunate soldiers went to the bottom, carried down by the weight of their equipment.

The sailors who were detailed to assist in the landing performed some heroic deeds. Theirs was the task of fixing the lighters from the gangways of the *River Clyde* to the shore. Even in ordinary times it would be a very difficult task, owing to the strong current which sweeps round from the Dardanelles, but to do it practically at the muzzle of the enemy's rifles demanded men with the hearts of lions. Scores were shot down as they tugged and hauled to get the lighters into position. Scores more were ready to jump into their places. More than once the lighters broke loose and the whole perilous work had to be done over again, but our gallant seamen never failed. They just "carried on."

Commander (now Captain) Unwin was awarded the Victoria Cross for fearlessly risking his life on more than one occasion in endeavouring to keep the lighters in position under the pitiless hail of lead.

Those naval men whose duty it was to bring the Dublins ashore in small boats were shot down to a man, for there was no escape for them from that terrible fire. Both boats and crew were destroyed, either on the beach, or before they reached it.

In spite of the rain of death some of the Dublins and Munsters succeeded in effecting a landing and making a dash for shelter from the tornado of fire under the little ridge of sand which, as I have already mentioned, ran round the beach. Had the Turks taken the precaution of levelling this bank of sand, not a soul could have lived in that fire-swept zone. More than half of the landing-party were killed before they could reach its friendly shelter and many others were left writhing in agony on that narrow strip of beach. Brigadier-General Napier and his Brigade Major, Captain Costeker, were killed, as was also Lieut.-Colonel Carrington Smith, commanding the Hampshires; the Adjutants of the Hampshires and of the Munsters were wounded and, indeed, the great majority of the senior officers were either wounded or killed.

Many anxious eyes were peering out over the protected bulwarks of the *River Clyde,* and among them was Father Finn, the Roman Catholic Chaplain of the Dublins. The sight of some five hundred of his brave boys lying dead or dying on that terrible strip of beach was too much for him, so, heedless of all risk, he plunged down the gangway and made for the shore. On the way, his wrist was shattered by a bullet, but he went on, and although lead was spattering all round him like hailstones, he administered consolation to the wounded and dying, who, alas! were so thickly strewn around. For a time he seemed to have had some miraculous form of Divine protection, for he went from one to another through shot and shell without receiving any further injury. At last a bullet struck him near the hip, and, on seeing this, some of the Dublins rushed out from the protection of the sandbank and brought him into its shelter. When, however, he had somewhat recovered from his wound, nothing would induce him to remain in safety while his poor boys were being done to death in the open, so out he crawled again to administer comfort to a poor fellow who was moaning piteously a little way off; and as he was in the act of giving consolation to the stricken man, this heroic Chaplain was struck dead by a merciful bullet.

Father Finn has, so far, been granted no V.C., but if there is such a thing in heaven, I am sure he is wearing it, and His Holiness Benedict XV might do worse than canonise this heroic priest, for surely no saint ever died more nobly: "Greater love hath no man than this, that a man lay down his life for his friends."

The Turkish position was so strong and they were able to pour down such a concentrated fire from pit, box, dress-circle, and gallery of their natural theatre, that every man of these gallant Irish regiments who showed himself in the open was instantly struck down. So hot and accurate was this close range Turkish fire that the disembarkation from the *River Clyde* had to be discontinued.

The little body of men who had escaped death and ensconced themselves under the sandbank kept up a lively fire on the Turks as long as their ammunition lasted, but there they had to remain for the best part of thirty-six hours, more or less at the mercy of the enemy. An attempt to dislodge them was, however, easily repelled by fire from the warships, as well as from the machine-guns on the decks of the *River Clyde*.

It was not until after nightfall that the remainder of the Irishmen could disembark, and then all the units had to be reorganised to enable them to make an attack on the formidable Turkish trenches on the following morning.

Practically every officer of the Dublins and Munsters was either killed or wounded, very few escaped scot free. The Dublins were particularly unfortunate, for at another landing-place, Camber Beach, close by Sedd-el-Bahr village, out of 125 men landed, only 25 were left at midday. Nevertheless, the fragments of the two battalions were pulled together by Lieut.-Colonel Doughty-Wylie and Lieut.-Colonel Williams, assisted by Captain Walford, R. A., Brigade Major. It will be readily understood what an arduous task it was to reorganise men who for over twenty-four hours had been subjected to the most murderous and incessant fire that ever troops had had to face; but nothing is impossible when really determined men make up their minds that it must be done, and early morning of the 26th April found the Dublins and Munsters and some of the Hampshires, led by Doughty-Wylie and Walford, dashing at the Turkish trenches, which they carried at the point of the bayonet. They rushed position after position, and by noon Sedd-el-Bahr village was in our hands, and here the gallant Walford was killed. Sedd-el-Bahr Castle yet remained to be taken, and it was while leading the final attack on the keep of this stronghold that the heroic Colonel Doughty-Wylie fell, mortally wounded, at the moment of victory. The posthumous honour of the Victoria Cross was granted to these two officers to commemorate their glorious deeds.

At the other landing-places the fighting had also been very fierce. At W Beach the Lancashire Fusiliers had a terribly difficult task in storming an almost impregnable position, which had been carefully prepared beforehand by the Turks. The high ground overlooking the beach had been strongly fortified with trenches; land mines and sea mines had been laid; wire entanglements extended round the shore and a barbed network had also been placed in the shallow water. Like V Beach it was a veritable death trap, but the brave Lancashires, after suffering terrible losses, succeeded in making good the landing and drove the Turks out of their trenches. In commemoration of their gallantry this Beach was afterwards known as Lancashire Landing.

The 2nd Battalion South Wales Borderers under Colonel Casson were able to land at S Beach, Morto Bay, and seize the high ground near De Tott's Battery, to which they tenaciously held on until the main body had driven the Turks back, when they joined hands with the troops from V Beach and continued the advance.

X Beach was stormed by the 1st Battalion Royal Fusiliers and part of the Anson Battalion Royal Naval Division, who drove before them such Turks as they found on the cliffs. They were reinforced by two more Battalions of the 87th Brigade, and after some heavy slogging they eventually got into touch with the Lancashire Fusiliers and Worcesters and so eased the pressure on V Beach by threatening the Turkish flank.

The landing on Y Beach was effected by the King's Own Scottish Borderers and the Plymouth Battalion of the Royal Marines. These splendid fellows forced their way into Krithia village, but want of ammunition and reinforcements obliged them to fall back to the beach, where they were almost overwhelmed by the enemy and lost more than half their numbers; eventually they were compelled to re-embark, but not before they had done immense damage to the Turks and considerably helped the troops who were forcing the other landings.

Meanwhile the two Australian-New Zealand Divisions were engaged in the perilous enterprise of forcing a landing in the face of a large Turkish force at a place now known as Anzac (this word being formed from the initial letters of Australian-New Zealand Army Corps). In the dark hour before the dawn some four thousand of these splendid fighters were towed in silence towards the shore, and here again it seemed as if they would meet with no opposition; but not so—the Turk was not to be caught napping, and, while the boats were still some way from land, thousands of Turkish soldiers rushed along the strip of beach to intercept the boats, and the heavy fire which they opened caused very severe casualties in the ranks; nothing, however, could daunt Colonel Maclagan and the men of the 3rd Australian Brigade; the moment the boats touched the shore these dare-devils leaped into the water and with irresistible fury drove the Turks before them at the point of the bayonet. Nothing could stand up against their onslaught, and by noon, having been reinforced, they had "hacked" their way some miles inland, put several Krupp guns out of action, and if they had been supported by even one more Division, the road to the Narrows would undoubtedly have been won. As it was, owing to lack of sufficient men to hold what they had made good, they were compelled to retire to the ridges overlooking the sea, and there for eight months they held the Turks at bay and hurled back, with frightful losses, every assault made on their position. Oh, if only the 29th Division had also been landed here, what a sweeping victory we would have won!

CHAPTER IX. THE ZION MULE CORPS LANDS IN GALLIPOLI

The beach, cliffs and Castle were now in our hands, and disembarkation for the remainder of the army was possible. While the great battle for the landing was going on, we had been fretting and fuming at being left so long idle spectators. Thinking that it was high time we should disembark, and finding that no orders came along for us, I felt that in order to get a move on I must make a personal effort. I therefore hailed a trawler which happened to be passing, and got it to take me over to the *Cornwallis*, on which I knew General Hunter-Weston, the Commander of the 29th Division, had his temporary headquarters.

The General was glad to see me, and said I had turned up just in the very nick of time, for my Zion men were urgently required ashore to take ammunition, food and water to the men in the firing line. He appealed to Admiral Wemyss, who was close by, to detail trawlers and lighters to get my Corps ashore as quickly as possible. The Admiral very kindly told off a naval officer to come with me, and he in his turn found a trawler and some horse boats which were soon alongside the *Dundrennon*.

From two to six o'clock P. M. we were busily employed loading up and sending mules and equipment ashore. I noticed that the officer in charge of our trawler was a bit of a bungler at his job; time after time he would fail in his judgment; when getting the barges alongside he had repeatedly to sail round and round the *Dundrennon* with his tow before he got near enough for a rope to be cast; he was not a regular naval man—just a "dug-out." How I longed then for my friend Murley!

I must say here that in my humble opinion the Navy failed us badly in the matter of tugs, lighters and horse boats; there were not nearly enough of these, and we could have done with three times the number. My Corps, which was most urgently wanted by the General, took three days to disembark, in spite of our most strenuous efforts to get ashore as quickly as possible. The delay was entirely due to the lack of tugs, for it was only now and then that a trawler could be spared to haul us inshore. We were sadly held up and kept waiting for hours after our boats had been loaded up, ready to be towed ashore.

Who was responsible for this shortage I do not know. It is, of course, quite possible that the Navy provided all the trawlers requisitioned for by the Army.

I had taken the precaution while on the ship to fill all my tins with fresh drinking water, and these had to be unloaded by hand from the lighters. To do this I arranged my men in a long line, stretching the whole length of the temporary pier from the lighters to the beach, and in this manner the cans of water were rapidly passed ashore from hand to hand.

While we were engaged on this work the guns from Asia were making very good shooting, shells striking the water within a few yards of us, just going over our heads, a little to the right or a little to the left, but always just missing. I watched my men very carefully to see how they would stand their baptism of fire, and I am happy to be able to say that, with one solitary exception, all appeared quite unconcerned and took not the slightest heed of the dangerous position they were in. The one exception was a youth from the *Yemen*, who trembled and chattered with nervousness; but when I went up to him, shook him somewhat ungently, and asked him what was the matter, he bent to his work and the cans passed merrily along. In fact, everybody there, especially the naval men who helped us to catch our mules as they jumped from the horse boats into the sea, treated the cannonade from Asia as a joke, and every time a shell missed a hearty laugh went up at the bad shooting of the Turkish gunners. It was only a mere fluke, however, that the shells did not hit the target aimed at, because, as a matter of fact, the shooting was particularly good and only missed doing a considerable amount of damage by a few yards each time. We were exceedingly fortunate in not losing a single man during the whole period of disembarkation.

Practically the first officer I met as I stepped ashore was Colonel Moorehouse, whom I had not seen for years, and he was most helpful in the present emergency. I found that he was in charge of the landing operations on the beach, and I believe he had given up a Governorship, or some such billet, in West Africa to do his bit in the Dardanelles.

While we were disembarking, General d'Amade, who was commanding the French Corps Expéditionnaire, stepped ashore and soon afterwards the French troops began to pour on to the beach.

During the great battle which took place on the 25th and 26th for the possession of V Beach, the French battleships and gunboats, together with the Russian cruiser *Askold*, had been battering down the fortress of Kum Kale on the Asiatic side of the Dardanelles, some two and a half miles in a direct line from Sedd-el-Bahr.

In the face of much opposition the French troops forced a landing, and after some heavy fighting defeated the Turks and captured many hundreds of prisoners. There is no doubt that this diversion averted much of the shell fire which would otherwise have been concentrated on those of us landing at V Beach. Having driven the Turks out and effectively destroyed Kum Kale, the French troops were re-embarked hurriedly, brought across the Dardanelles, landed at V Beach in feverish haste, and flung into the thick of the fight which was still raging just north of the village of Sedd-el-Bahr.

I watched them disembark, and it was magnificent to see the verve and dash which the French gunners displayed in getting their beloved .75s into action.

Our naval men helped to bring the guns ashore, but the moment the Frenchmen got them there they had them away and in action on the ridge to the north of the amphitheatre in an incredibly short space of time.

As soon as we had got a couple of hundred mules ashore, I was ordered to march them off to W Beach, which was on the western side of Cape Helles. Having had some experience of the ways of soldiers on active service, I knew that we should have to keep a very sharp eye on our gear as it came ashore, otherwise it would be appropriated by the first comer. I therefore left Lieutenant Claude Rolo on the beach to look after the mules, horses and stores as they were disembarked, and incidentally to dodge the shells which more than once covered him with sand but did no further damage. I had left Lieutenant Gye on board the *Dundrennon* to see to the work of loading up the barges.

On the way to W Beach we were fired on by Turkish riflemen who had not as yet been driven very far away from the shore, but fortunately we sustained no damage.

The Lancashire Fusiliers, as I have already described, had a terribly difficult task in forcing their way on to W Beach, and the moment I saw it I could well realise what an arduous undertaking it must have been. It looked, like V Beach, an impossibility, but the Lancashire lads could not be denied, and all honour to them for having stormed such a fearsome stronghold. By the time I got there there was already a huge stock of ammunition and supplies piled up on the shore, and these we at once began to load up on the mules to take out to the men in the firing line, who were constantly driving the Turks before them further and further from the beach.

I shall never forget my first night in Gallipoli. We loaded up a couple of hundred mules, each mule carrying about two thousand cartridges, and with Major O'Hara (now Lieut.-Colonel O'Hara), who was the D. A. Q. M. G., as guide, we marched off into the darkness to distribute ammunition along the front.

Major O'Hara came with me, partly because he knew the way, and partly because he wanted to make sure what were the most urgent needs of the men in the trenches. We trudged together all through that trying night, so it is not much to be wondered at that we almost quarrelled once or twice—but I will say here that of all the men I met in Gallipoli there was not one who was so capable at his job, or worked so hard to see that everything for which he was responsible ran smoothly. Oh, if only our Army could be staffed with O'Haras, what a wonderfully efficient machine our Army would be!

Soon after we left W Beach in the dark it began to pour, and it poured and poured solidly for about five hours.

On we squelched through the mud over unknown tracks with the water streaming down our bodies and running in rivulets out of our boots. As soon as the rain ceased a biting cold wind set in, which froze us to the marrow. However, the vigorous walking, helping up a fallen mule, readjusting the loads, getting out of holes into which we had tumbled, etc., kept our circulation going, and when we arrived at a place known as Pink Farm, the furthest point to which we had yet advanced, there was a sudden alarm that the Turks were approaching. Nobody knew then where our front line was, or whether it linked up across the Peninsula. There were many gaps in it through which the Turks, if they had had initiative enough, might have forced their way and inflicted a considerable amount of damage upon us before we could have organised adequate resistance.

On the first alarm of the approaching Turks I sent a man out to reconnoitre, formed my little escort in open order, prone on the grass, and asked Major Moore, D. S. O. of the General Staff, now Brigadier-General Moore, to bring some men from the trenches, if he could find them, as quickly as possible, for I had no desire to lose my convoy at such an early stage of the proceedings.

Gongs could plainly be heard sounding, apparently close by, as though it was some prearranged signal of the enemy, but whatever the reason we saw nothing of the Turks, and no attack was made, so we unloaded our ammunition and were then sent back for more by Colonel B. to Lancashire Landing. Now Colonel B. of the Headquarters Staff told me personally on no account to bring back supplies, but only ammunition, as no supplies were needed at this place for the present. Unluckily O'Hara was not on the spot when Colonel B. gave me these explicit and reiterated instructions, so when we got back to the beach he wished to load up supplies, but this I refused to do owing to the specific orders I had received. O'Hara was furious but I was obdurate, so, of course, we loaded up with ammunition.

Back again we trudged steadily through rain and slush towards the Pink Farm. When we had got about half-way, we were met by a Staff Officer who told us,—to O'Hara's great satisfaction,—that it was not ammunition which was now wanted at the Pink Farm but supplies. I am not at all sure that I did not overhear O'Hara call me "an obstinate damn fool," but it is as well to be hard of hearing as it is to possess a blind eye on occasions.

The upshot was that we had to return to the beach, unload the ammunition, load up boxes of tinned beef, cheese, biscuits and jam, and then back again along the "sludgy squdgy" road we trudged once more towards that never-to-be-forgotten Pink Farm. Again we got about half-way there, when yet another Staff Officer met us, who told us that the supplies were not wanted by the brigade holding the line at the Pink Farm, but by the brigade holding the line on the extreme right, where they were urgently required, and he ordered us to take them there without delay. It was now my turn to chuckle, and I observed to O'Hara that there "really must be a damn fool somewhere about after all."

Without a murmur we turned back once more, for, not knowing the country, nor where we might bump into the enemy, we could not take a short cut across, so were forced to return to W Beach. From thence we went along the track by the Helles cliff which took us to the top of V Beach; our route then led us through Sedd-el-Bahr village, where we were warned by a French soldier that we would be sniped by Turks as there were many still lurking there.

When we got safely clear of this jumpy place, we found ourselves wending our way through some Turkish cemeteries, the tall, white, thin headstones, with their carved headlike top knobs, looking exactly like ghosts in the gloomy light. We passed through cypress groves, along sandy lanes, and rugged paths, fell into and scrambled out of dug-outs, ditches and dongas, where mules and loads tumbled about indiscriminately to the accompaniment of much profanity.

At one spot on this adventurous journey we came upon a Battalion of Zouaves crouching down for rest and shelter in the lee of a hedge. The sergeant in charge of my escort took them for Turks, and only that I was happily on the spot when he made this startling discovery, he would undoubtedly have opened fire on the Frenchmen. I must say that they looked exactly like Turks, owing to their semi-barbaric uniform.

When we got the convoy to where we thought the front line ought to be, we failed to find it, and as we were very hazy as to whether we would run into our own men or the Turks, we left the convoy under the cover of some trees, and O'Hara and I went off to reconnoitre. I believe we must have passed through a gap in our own line. At all events we wandered for some time, making many pauses to listen for any sound that might guide us, but the weird thing about it was, that the whole place was now still as death, though we must have been quite close to both armies. No doubt they were dead beat after the recent terrific fighting they had come through.

At last we luckily struck our own men, lining a shallow trench which had apparently been very hastily thrown up, for it scarcely afforded enough cover to shelter a decent-sized terrier. The men were so exhausted with the continued strain and stress of the battle, which had been continuous since the morning of the 25th, that they slept as if they were dead. The sentries, of course, were on the alert, looking out grim and watchful at the Turkish line, which we could just make out in the struggling moonlight, apparently not more than two hundred yards away.

Telling the sentinel in a low voice, so as not to draw the Turkish fire, that we had brought up a convoy of supplies, and that we were about to unload them among some trees a couple of hundred yards further back, we ordered him to pass this information on to the Brigade Headquarters, so that arrangements might be made for the distribution of the food before daybreak.

We then turned back, and taking the mules out of the shelter of the trees where we had left them, we brought the supplies as close as possible to the firing line, where we stacked them under cover.

Here again O'Hara's thoroughness and readiness to help in all things came out, for he was one of the busiest men in the convoy, helping to unload, putting the boxes in order, and removing our pack-ropes from the cases, for, of course, these always had to be untied and taken back with the mules.

We saw some pathetic sights on our way back to W Beach; we were obliged to stop every now and again so as not to bump into the wounded men who were being carried down on stretchers to the ships all night long by the devoted R. A. M. C. orderlies.

When we topped the crest overlooking W Beach, a gleam of light was coming up out of Asia, telling us of the approach of dawn, and we felt, as we wearily strode down the slope to the beach, that we had done a hard and useful night's work.

Now, when I had disembarked from the *Dundrennon* soon after midday, I had no idea that I would be hustled off to the trenches at an instant's notice. I had expected to go back to the ship again for at least one more load of mules, and I had therefore nothing with me except what I stood up in—no food or equipment of any kind, and beyond a dry biscuit and some cheese, I had had nothing to eat since lunch-time, so that it can be well imagined I was fairly ravenous when I had finished that night's trek. There was no food to be had just yet, however, and in any case I had to see to the watering and feeding of my mules, for they, like myself, had been without food or drink since the previous midday.

This job was finished by about 7 A. M. and soon after that I joined O'Hara at an excellent breakfast, after which I felt ready for another strenuous day.

CHAPTER X. A NIGHT UP THE GULLY RAVINE

Feeling greatly refreshed after my breakfast with O'Hara, I went to select a suitable place for our camp, or rather bivouac, for, of course, we had no tents. Finding a snug little valley which stood back a couple of hundred yards from W Beach and which ran up under the protection of a rise in the ground, which gave us some slight cover from the Turks, I put all hands on to prepare and level the ground for the horse and mule lines.

We had been rushed to the trenches in such haste with the ammunition and supplies that we had been unable to bring any rope with which to tether the mules, so, seeing some ship's rope lying on the beach, I asked the naval officer in charge to let me have it for my lines. He not only did this, but lent me some of his men as well to carry it up to my little camp, where they helped me to fix it in the ground. I am sorry to say I forget this officer's name, as he was most helpful to me in many ways, and I never had to appeal in vain to him, or, as a matter of fact, to any other naval officer for assistance.

Throughout the day there was more than enough to do. The ground had to be levelled off, so as to make comfortable the mule and horse lines. Ropes had to be pegged down and the ends of them buried in the ground, tied round sacks filled with clay, drains trenched out, and the larger stones thrown out of the way. Then the mules had to be fed and watered, and I feared the latter was going to be a difficult and dangerous business, for the only water discovered so far came under Turkish fire. Luckily for me, however, one of my men, Schoub, my farrier sergeant, discovered a deep well carefully hidden at the corner of a demolished building, standing at the head of the little valley where we were camped. I feared that it might have been poisoned, so to solve my doubts I went to the Provost Marshal, and borrowed from him one of the captured Turkish prisoners. I felt sure that a Turk coming from these parts would know the natural taste of the water, so I took him with me to the well and asked him to drink. He was rather loth to do this at first, but at last, with a little persuasion, he took a sip in his mouth, rolled it for a moment on his tongue, then, nodding approval, drank freely of the water. As he survived the ordeal, I thought it was all right to go ahead with the mules, and later on we used the well ourselves, for it was excellent water.

All day long parties were coming and going between V and W Beaches; forage, water tins, supplies, etc.—everything had to be brought to us on our pack mules, and the day was all too short to do the many things that landing in a new country in time of warfare makes necessary. Not much time was wasted over the cooking of food; biscuits, jam, cheese, tinned beef, required no fires; only a little tea was boiled in our hastily-made camp kitchens. The only fuel to be had was obtained by breaking up some of our old packing-cases; the Turks had cleared off everything—not a man, woman, child or beast was left on the place—but this did not worry us, as we were always able to rustle for ourselves.

Before dark that night we began to load up another big convoy of munitions and supplies for the trenches.

This proved to be one of the most weird nights of many that we have spent tramping up and down the peninsula.

Of course, we had to move off after dark, otherwise the Turks would have concentrated their artillery on us and we should all have been destroyed. We went from W to X Beach, along the Ægean shore, falling into trenches and dug-outs on the way, for the night was very dark, while every now and again we were caught up in Turkish wire entanglements. Then from X Beach we slowly pioneered our way through the trackless scrub and undergrowth until we came to the cliff which overlooks Gully Beach, at the mouth of a huge ravine which here opened into the Ægean Sea, some miles northwest of W Beach.

On the way we had to go through some of our own guns, which were in action on this side of the Peninsula, and I had to request the Battery Commander to cease fire while we were filing past, as I feared the roar and flash of the guns might stampede the mules. He let us through in silence, but we had scarcely got fifty yards from the muzzles when out belched the guns again, the roar of which at such close range, to my surprise, did not in the least upset the mules. I shall never forget our struggling down to the sea from the cliffs above the Gully. Of course there was no road then and we had to reconnoitre ahead in the dark every yard of the way. Often I had to turn back and call out to the men to halt as I found myself dangling on the edge of the cliff, holding on to the roots of the gorse, which fortunately grew there in profusion. After many mishaps, mules and supplies falling about among the ravines which scored the face of the cliff, we eventually reached the beach.

Then began our march up the bed of the ravine, and although the Gully was very wide and there was ample room to march either to right or left of the stream, yet we knew nothing of this, for the ground was new to us and everything was pitch dark, so the only sure way of getting up the ravine in safety was to walk in the river bed. I led the way, expecting all the time either to fall into a waterhole or be shot by an ambuscade of Turks. Cliffs loomed up on either side of us to a height of a hundred or more feet, and there was nothing to be seen but the faint twinkle of the stars overhead.

Now and again I called a halt to reconnoitre and listen for any suspicious movements ahead, as it was a most likely spot in which to be ambushed by the enemy. So far as I knew the Turks were in possession of the bank to my left, and all that part of the country right up to Anzac, where the Australians had landed. For a time everything was quiet as we splashed our way along, there being a lull just then in the fighting; all of a sudden it broke out again with feverish intensity. The Gully Ravine made a turn at one part of its course which took us right between the line of fire of the two opposing forces. Shells from our own guns screamed and passed safely over the ravine, but the shells from the Turkish batteries often burst exactly overhead, scattering shrapnel all round, at other times plunking into the cliff on our right and smothering us with clay and gravel. The rattle of musketry was like the continuous roll of kettledrums, and considering all our surroundings, and the fierce fight that was going on, it was altogether a night to be remembered.

At last we reached the troops holding the front line; there were no supports or reserves, so far as I could see; every man had been put into the firing line, owing to the terrible losses that had been sustained.

Here in the dark, with shot and shell flying all round, we unpacked our mules and handed over the ammunition and food to the brigade.

I was right glad to be able to turn back and get my convoy safely away from the gloomy depths of this uncanny ravine.

We had again to climb the cliffs when we got back to the sea at the gully-mouth, and at the top again to negotiate our guns, which were still blazing away for all they were worth. However, by dint of much shouting when I had crawled close enough to be heard, the gunners ceased fire just long enough to enable us to slip through.

These two nights are fair examples of the work done in those early days by the Zion Mule Corps, at that time the only transport corps on the Peninsula at Helles.

CHAPTER XI. HOW ZION MULES UPSET TURKISH PLANS

It will be remembered that I left Claude Rolo on V Beach to take charge of our gear as it came off the *Dundrennon*, while Gye was left aboard that vessel to hurry everything ashore; but it was not until the third day that we had disembarked all our belongings, the delay being entirely due to the shortage of steam tugs, on which I have already commented.

During the time that our gear was stacked on V Beach, with, of course, a guard in charge of it, one of the sentries became the object of suspicion to the French, who were now in entire control of V Beach. After a few minutes, finding he could speak no understandable language (for he only spoke Russian or Hebrew, which, no doubt, sounded Turkish to the French), and seeing that he was armed with a Turkish rifle and bayonet and had Turkish cartridges in his belt, he was taken for a daring Turk who had invaded the beach to spy out the land. Without more ado, he was tried by drum-head court-martial and condemned to be shot out of hand. He was actually up against the walls of Sedd-el-Bahr Castle, and the firing party in position to carry out the execution, when the Sergeant in charge of the Zionist Guard luckily spied what was happening, and, as he spoke excellent French, he rapidly explained the situation. The man was released, but the shock was too much for him, and when he was unbound he was found to be paralysed, and it was two months before he was fit for duty again. After this, I allowed none of my men to leave camp unless they could speak English or were accompanied by some one who could act as interpreter.

Gye and Rolo worked hard to move the pile of equipment—water tins, forage, etc., etc., to the little valley where the rest of the Corps were already snugly encamped, overlooking W Beach. I was extremely glad to have these two officers with me again, because, during these three days and nights since the landing, while we were separated, I had had a very strenuous time.

I remember when Gye saw me for the first time after coming ashore, he got quite a shock, and I believe he must have imagined that I had been indulging in some frightful orgy, because he observed that the whites of my eyes were as red as burning coals; but it was only an orgy of work and want of sleep.

I may say that when I did sleep I slept very soundly indeed, for a high explosive shell dropped within seven or eight feet of my head, exploded, blew a great hole in the ground, yet I never even heard it!

This feat was outdone by a man who, on being roused in the morning, found himself lame, and then discovered that he had been shot through the foot some time in the night, while asleep!

The work, owing to Gye and Rolo being with me, was now considerably lightened, as we each took a convoy out to different parts of the front, and so got the distribution of supplies through much more quickly. I was unable at that time to make use of my Jewish officers, with the exception of Captain Trumpledor, for they were without experience and could not speak English. Later on they were able to take charge of convoys and did the work very well.

Gye, Rolo and I made a cheery little party and never found the time hang heavy on our hands, nor were we ever dull for a moment, even when we returned from convoy work at two o'clock in the morning. We would then have dinner together, and Gye was such a wonderful story-teller, and Claude Rolo was such a good second, and he also possessed such an infectious laugh, that I have often literally fallen from the box on which I was sitting, convulsed with merriment. I am sure the men of L Battery, R. H. A., who were camped close by, must have wondered what all this unseemly racket was about at such unearthly hours of the morning.

Gye's knowledge of colloquial Arabic was profound. It is related of him in Egypt that a Cairo street loafer on one occasion maliciously annoyed him, whereupon Gye turned upon him and let loose such a flood of Arabic slang, minutely vituperating the fellow himself and his ancestors for fourteen generations back, that, despairing of ever reaching such heights of eloquence, the loafer, out of sheer envy, went straight away and hanged himself!

In this first little bivouac of ours I spread my ground sheet and blanket in the corner of what had been a house. The guns of the Fleet had evidently got on to it and now nothing was left standing but some of the walls, which in places were about three or four feet high.

A day or two after settling in here I happened to jump down from one of these walls and the ground gave way somewhat under me. We made an excavation into it and discovered, hidden away in an underground chamber, an old green silk flag, so ancient that a touch rent it, an antiquated battle-axe dating, I should say, from the time of the Crusaders, and also some antique brass candlesticks—a curious and rare find in such a place.

It must not be supposed that the Turks left us in peace during the day. They constantly dropped shells into our little valley, tearing holes in the ground all round us, but by great good fortune while we were in this place we suffered no casualty of any kind, either man or mule.

On May 1st, after nightfall, I sent Claude Rolo out in the direction of the Gully Ravine, with ammunition and supplies for one of the Brigades of the 29th Division. He got to his destination safely, but while he was unloading the convoy, at about ten o'clock, whether by chance or design I know not, a tremendous hail of shrapnel was poured upon them from the Turkish guns a couple of miles away. Some forty of the mules had already been relieved of their loads and many of these broke away and galloped off into the darkness.

This turned out to be a providential diversion, for they helped to save the British Army that night, in much the same way as the cackling geese once saved Rome, for, all unknown to us, masses of Turks were at that very moment creeping up in the dark just before the rise of the moon. They were in three lines, the first line being without ammunition, as it was their particular business, when they got near enough to our trenches, to rush them with the bayonet. The Turkish General Staff, however, had not calculated on Zion mules! The terrified animals, scared and wounded by the shrapnel, careered over our trenches and clattered down with clanking chains on the stealthy foe. The Turks undoubtedly took them for charging cavalry, for they poured a volley into them and thus gave away their position.

Our men instantly lined the trenches and opened such an intense fire that the Turks were utterly routed, and those of them that were left alive fled back to the cover of their own trenches. The battle was taken up all along the line, and, if volume of musketry counts for anything, it was the hottest night fight we had during all the time we were on the Peninsula.

Claude Rolo had a most arduous and perilous time collecting his men and mules in the midst of all this turmoil, but he eventually got them together and took them down a side track to the Gully, into which they all scrambled helter-skelter, for safety.

One of the men, Private Groushkousky, distinguished himself greatly in this fight, for when the hail of shrapnel descended on the convoy and stampeded many of the mules, this plucky boy—for he was a mere youth—although shot through both arms, held on to his plunging animals and safely delivered his loads of ammunition to the men in the firing line. I promoted Private Groushkousky to the rank of Corporal, for his pluck and devotion to duty, and, in addition, recommended him for the D. C. M., which I am glad to say he obtained.

While Rolo and his men were having such a strenuous time on the left of the line, I took a convoy to the Brigade holding the centre. At about two o'clock in the morning, soon after we had returned, we were all having a much-needed sleep, for we were worn out with constant coming and going day and night. I was roused from a deep slumber into which I had fallen by a messenger to say ammunition was urgently required by the Anson Battalion of the Royal Naval Division and other units on the right flank of our line. I remember what a difficult task it was to rouse the men, who lay about on the ground, like rolled-up balls, in front of their mules. I found a very effective plan was to shout loudly in their ear: "Turks!" That, coupled with the roar of the guns and the crackling of the rifles, quickly brought them back to realities, and almost in the twinkling of an eye the Zion men were loading up cartridges with feverish speed at the Ordnance Depot, which was situated not many yards below our lines. I always kept our mules saddled throughout the day and night, in relays, for I knew that in those strenuous times I would be likely to get a call at any moment to supply the firing line with ammunition.

No matter at what hour of the day or night we went to the ammunition stack, Major Howell Jones, the Chief Ordnance Officer of the 29th Division, was always on the spot to issue it; and not only was he there, but if there was any "push" on, he turned to and helped to load up the mules with his own hands. He was one of the hardest-worked men on the Peninsula, and I sincerely hope that the 29th Division realises all it owes to his energy and foresight.

In those early days after the first landing, when we were pressing the Turks so steadily before us, and we all expected that one final push would drive them over Achi Baba, the Zionists petitioned General Hunter-Weston to be permitted to take part in the assault. After some consideration, the General refused to let us go, saying that we were performing invaluable services in keeping the men in the trenches supplied with ammunition and food. Although we were denied officially the privilege of actually taking part in the attack, yet unofficially some of the Corps, at least, had the gratification of joining battle with the Turks.

It must be remembered that our troops had suffered terrible losses in those early battles, and the Inniskilling Fusiliers had fared no better than the rest, and they had very few men indeed with which to man their trenches in the event of an attack. Now it so happened that the Turks made a determined onslaught upon them on one occasion, when a party of the Zion Mule Corps was close by, unloading a convoy; and these Zionists, having the lust of battle strong in them, and seeing how weak the Inniskillings were, left their mules to take care of themselves and, under the leadership of Corporal Hildersheim, leaped into the trenches and materially assisted in repelling the Turks.

CHAPTER XII. LIFE IN OUR NEW CAMP

More and more troops kept on disembarking and within fourteen days we found ourselves being crowded out of our little valley that ran up from the sea, and it became a pressing necessity to look out for fresh quarters further inland. Nor were we sorry to move, for a road had been made close to our lines, which, owing to the great traffic upon it, was now several inches deep in fine white dust, which blew over us in choking clouds.

At this time, the whole of the Peninsula, from Cape Helles to Achi Baba, was one expanse of green pastures and cultivation, and the country looked exceedingly pretty. Quantities of beautiful flowers grew everywhere, so much so that some fields were a regular blaze of colour, the western slopes of Achi Baba itself being beautified by gorgeous stretches of blood-red poppies. Groves of trees of various kinds were dotted about, while the olive and the almond flourished everywhere. Here and there were to be seen round, masonry-topped wells, just like those pictured in illustrated Bibles, showing Rebecca drawing water for Abraham's servant—but, alas, here there was no Rebecca!

Before we left it, this smiling land became the most desolate, God-forsaken place that it is possible to imagine—nothing but row upon row of unsightly trenches, and not a single blade of grass anywhere to meet the eye.

For our new encampment I chose a level green field, some two miles inland, and into this we moved on May 11th.

A beautiful olive tree grew and threw a grateful shade by the edge of our encampment, and here, practically under its roots, we excavated a shallow dug-out and erected over it a shelter of canvas. Gye, Rolo and I settled ourselves in as comfortably as possible, and although we thought it merely a temporary halting-place on the way to Constantinople, we never moved camp again, and, indeed, for over seven months it was our home.

I had occasion to ride back to W Beach within a couple of hours after quitting our first encampment, and I heartily congratulated myself that we had cleared out of it just in the nick of time, for the Turks had concentrated their guns on the place immediately after we had left. I counted no less than thirty holes through a piece of canvas that was stretched over the place where we had slept the night before. Had we still been there we must all inevitably have been blown to smithereens!

At our new encampment we found, burrowed into the ground about us, the wagon lines of B, L and Y Batteries, R. H. A., together with the ammunition column—in fact, our lines joined up with L Battery, which, it will be remembered, earned such fame, and won so many V.C.'s during the retreat from Mons. Lieutenant Davidson of this Battery was in charge of the wagon lines, and, as it was Gallipoli, and he was all alone, the haughty horse gunner did not disdain to join the lowly Muleteers' Mess! We were very glad to have him, as he was good, cheery, sensible company, and he also made a fourth at Bridge, which was our relaxation when nothing else had to be done. It is odd, when one thinks of it now, that we were far more interested at times, when the game got exciting, as to who should make the odd trick than in the Turkish shells, which flew screaming by a few feet over our heads, especially when one remembers that the deflection of the guns by a hair's-breadth by those tiresome fellows who were peppering us from Achi Baba and the plains of Ilium would have meant that, in our peaceful little dug-out, spades would have been trumps!

During the course of our stay here we gradually excavated and enlarged our dwelling and burrowed down into the ground, making a cellar into which we could retire in case the shelling became too hot, but, as a matter of fact, though the bombardment at times was hot enough to satisfy the most desperate fire-eater, we used our bomb proof entirely as a pantry, for which we found it most useful.

No sooner had we settled down to life in our new bivouac than the Turks began to annoy us by dropping shells into it and disturbing our peace of mind and body. On the morning following our arrival, while we were having breakfast under the spreading branches of our olive tree, a shrapnel burst, sending its bullets unpleasantly near. I remarked jocularly to the others that if the next shell came any closer we should have to move. Scarcely had I spoken when one went bang just over us, and a bullet whizzed between our heads and smashed through the arm of my Orderly Room Sergeant, Abulafia, who at that moment was standing by my side taking some orders. It is a marvel how it missed hitting a member of our little mess, for we were all sitting very close together round an upturned box which we were using as a breakfast table.

The same shell wounded two other men, besides killing and wounding half a dozen mules. We decided that the place was too hot for us, so, after helping our Medical Officer to dress the wounded, we finished our breakfast on the other side of a bank which ran along by our olive tree.

I must mention here that Sergeant Abulafia refused to have his wound dressed until the others who were more seriously injured had first received attention.

Dr. Levontin was very good in attending to wounded men under fire, and he gave first aid to these men and many others, often at great personal risk; but at last the continual battering of high explosive shells so close to his dug-out was too much for him, and his nerves went, as did the nerves of many others, and there was nothing for it but to send him back to Egypt. From the time of his departure our sick and wounded were ministered to by Captain Blandy, R. A. M. C., who was the medical officer in charge of the batteries camped round us, and the men, finding Captain Blandy most sympathetic and painstaking, did not fail to avail themselves to the full of his able services.

The troublesome Turks did not allow us to keep our animals in the pleasant field where we had, after much trouble, laid down our ropes and pegs and made our lines.

From Achi Baba and the slopes above Krithia they could see us perfectly well, and they rained such a tornado of shells round about us, ploughing up the ground in all directions, that I ordered a hasty evacuation of the field and chose another site close by, somewhat better concealed from view by a plantation of olive trees. It was extremely difficult to hide from the Turks as Achi Baba dominated the whole Peninsula. Even in our new position we were not allowed to remain undisturbed, for almost daily the Turks peppered us with shrapnel and high explosives, both from Achi Baba and the Asiatic coast.

I set the men to work to dig themselves and the mules well into the bowels of the earth, and in a very short time they had done this so effectually that a stranger visiting the place would be astonished if he were told that some hundreds of men and mules were concealed right under his very nose.

Soon after we had evacuated the field in which the Turks had shelled us so vigorously it was taken possession of by the Collingwood Battalion of the Royal Naval Division. They arrived in the dusk of the evening, and as they were apparently unaware of their dangerous position, I felt it to be my duty to go and warn the Commanding Officer, Captain Spearman, R. N., how exposed the place was, and how they would probably be plastered by high explosives as soon as the Turks discovered them on the following morning. Captain Spearman was very glad to be given this friendly warning and, in consequence, he made his Battalion dig itself well in, and for several hours into the night I could hear pick and spade digging and delving. It was well they did so, for on the following morning a brisk bombardment opened on them, but, thanks to the precautions which they had taken, they, on that day at all events, suffered no casualties.

It was very funny to see the men sitting in rows along the banks of earth thrown up out of their "dug-outs" and watch them dive, like rabbits into their burrows, at the sound of an approaching shell; then, after the explosion, every one popped up again to see what damage had been done.

During the time they were camped there a shell would now and again plump right into a dug-out and then, of course, the unfortunate occupants would be blown about in little pieces all over the place. A hand was once blown down to my horse lines, some hundred and fifty yards away from where the shell had burst, and shattered a man to atoms.

A German Taube for a time flew over our lines every morning long before sunrise, of course catching all our airmen napping. These visits were generally for observation purposes, but sometimes the Taubes would liven us up by dropping a few bombs. They made several shots at the French guns, but always missed. I saw a bomb land among a dozen French horses one day, and all of the unfortunate animals were terribly wounded. I never saw such shambles, for the horses were in a dug-out close together for safety. The Zion lines had several close escapes, as did the Royal Naval Division Hospital which was close to us, and where Staff-Surgeon Fleming cheerfully and skilfully attended to our sick and wounded at all times of the day and night.

The Taube is a much more vicious looking machine than ours. It has a certain air of arrogance about it, entirely lacking in our type of aeroplane. It is not in the least like a dove, as the German name signifies, but appears to me very like a hawk, always ready to pounce on its prey.

Day by day one kept missing friendly faces. I remember such a nice boy, belonging to one of the Naval Battalions, who used to pass my camp regularly with his platoon on his way to the beach to bathe. I never knew the boy's name, but he interested me as he was a bright, cheery, handsome youngster, who seemed to be on the best of terms with his men. One day there was a vigorous bombardment of his lines, and when next the platoon went by the young officer was missing. He had been blown to pieces by a shell.

The Royal Naval Division were a mixed crowd, and their ways in Gallipoli were somewhat peculiar. Their habits and customs were decidedly "herumphroditish." They performed military duties as ordinary Infantry; then they jumped back and were sailors again. They kept time by the chiming of ships' bells; when they were wanted out of their dug-outs the boatswain would pipe "All hands on deck"; when a company was mustered on parade, the Commander (when the Commodore came along!) reported "All present on the main deck, sir"—the main deck being along a line of dug-outs; and if one herumphrodite wished to visit another herumphrodite in a different Battalion, he had to apply for "shore leave"!

The Collingwood Battalion met with a very sad end soon after their arrival in my neighbourhood. They were sent up to take part for the first time in an attack on the Turkish trenches, and they were placed on our extreme right, linking up with the French. When the order came to charge, they went forward most gallantly, capturing, with little loss, two of the Turkish lines of trenches, Captain Spearman, well to the fore, leading his men. He got shot in the foot, but, ignoring it, dashed along, waving his hat in the air as he cheered his men to the assault. Unfortunately, owing to the conspicuous part he and his officers played in the attack (and it was necessary that they should do so, owing to the rawness of the men), he and practically all the other officers of the battalion were killed. Then some one, possibly a German, for there were several of them in the Turkish trenches round about, shouted out the fatal word "Retire." This was carried along the line and the men turned about and made back, helter-skelter, for their own trenches, but in trying to gain them they were practically annihilated by machine-gun and rifle fire. I was particularly sorry for Captain Spearman, who had come to our dug-out on many occasions, and had drunk an early cup of coffee with us only a few hours before he was killed.

In this disastrous retreat the Collingwood Battalion was practically wiped out. The survivors were transferred to another unit of the Royal Naval Division and the very name of this Battalion went out of existence.

CHAPTER XIII. A MAY BATTLE

During a big battle which took place early in May, I sent Gye forward with a large convoy of ammunition, and on riding out later on to see how things were going I passed over some of the ground occupied by the French, who were to the right of the British, and extended from thence across the Peninsula to the Dardanelles. A couple of miles to the rear of the fighting line extended the batteries of the famous .75s, cunningly concealed among trees, branches specially planted in the ground, reeds, etc. I watched the gunners serve their guns, and my admiration was aroused at witnessing the ease and celerity with which they were loaded, their mechanical arrangement for setting the fuse, and, above all, the beautifully smooth recoil of the barrel. This was so nicely adjusted that I might have placed my finger on the ground behind the wheel of the gun and have received no damage.

The French Army can give us points on many things, but above all stands their .75 gun. They are wonderfully accurate, marvellously quick, and seem able to pour out from their muzzles a continuous stream of projectiles. The French certainly did not starve their gunners in ammunition, and only for those .75s our position in Gallipoli would often have been somewhat precarious.

After I had watched the guns in action for a while I passed on, and going down the sandy road which led from Sedd-el-Bahr village to Krithia I came upon the first evidences of the fight that was now raging. A handsome young French artilleryman lay dead by the side of the road; some friend had closed his eyes, and he looked as if he merely slept, but it was the long sleep of death. A little further on lay some Zouaves, and yet a little further some Senegalese, all lying just as they fell, with their packs on their backs and their rifles close by, facing the foe—brave French soldiers all.

Turning a corner I found myself riding into General d'Amade and his staff, busily directing the battle. Almost at the General's horse's feet lay a Turk whose face was half blown away. The poor fellow had wrapped the end of his pugaree round his ghastly wound. Within a yard or two lay another Turk, his shoulder smashed to pulp by a shell. Both men bore up with the greatest fortitude and never uttered a groan. A first-aid dressing station was close by, where scores of wounded, French and Turks, were being doctored and bandaged. These sights of the uglier and sadder side of war are not pleasing, and any one who has seen the horrors of it can never wish to view such scenes again. I would put all Foreign Ministers, Diplomats and Newspaper Proprietors in the forefront of every battle for which they were in any way responsible. However, duty has to be done, even in the midst of horrors, so saluting the General, I pushed further along to the front, where I could see Gye with the mules in the distance.

By the time I had cantered up to him all the ammunition had been unloaded, and at the spot where I halted I found myself looking over a bank into the midst of a Battalion of cheery little Gurkhas (the 6th) and almost within handshake of their Commander, Colonel C. Bruce, who was an old acquaintance of mine. I had no idea he was in Gallipoli, and it was curious to come upon him, after some years, in the thick of a battle.

I stayed for a time chatting with him while the bullets and shells whizzed round—in fact, until an order came for his Battalion to go forward into the fight.

I myself went and took up a position on a hill close by, where I could see, as if from the gallery of a theatre, the whole fight staged before me; where I could note the move of practically every man and gun.

As I looked down from my post of observation, a saucer-like green valley full of olive trees, vine-yards and young corn spread out before me for some five miles, right away up to Achi Baba, the dominating hill, some six hundred or seven hundred feet high. The French, as I have already said, were away on the right, and I watched their infantry mass in hollows and ravines, then advance in wavy lines under the pounding shelter of their guns. The latter were served magnificently, and the infantry as they advanced found the ground to their immediate front swept yard by yard by the guns fired by their comrades a couple of miles to their rear.

It was a stirring sight to watch the officers dash out and give the men a lead when there was any hesitation or waver of the line. In places I could see the Turks run like hares, but on the extreme left the French who were in touch with our right could be seen retiring precipitately over the hill, badly slated by the Turks.

I was fascinated by the sight and wondered how that broken line could be again reformed. It was done, however, in the shelter of a bluff, and once more they charged over the hill and were then lost to my view.

The 29th Division extended from the French left, near the right centre of the saucer, across to the Ægean Sea. The front was towards Achi Baba, and our men made headway towards it in the face of fierce opposition. Our guns were barking away at the Turks in their trenches, and the great guns of the Fleet were hurling their high explosives, which descended on the doomed Turks with terrific effect. One could see great spurts of flame, smoke, earth, timbers, rocks, Turks, in fact, everything in the neighbourhood, going up as though shot out of the crater of a volcano.

To me it seemed as though nothing could possibly live under such a reign of death, which continued with ever-increasing intensity for an hour. Nothing could be seen of Achi Baba, or any other part of the Turkish position, owing to the smoke and dust which the bombardment had raised, and unfortunately the wind was blowing towards us, which brought everything into the eyes of our men as they leaped out of the trenches to the attack.

The moment the guns ceased one could discern, through the haze, the gleam of bayonets as the Allies swept forward along the whole front like a bristling wall of steel, right into the leading Turkish trenches.

Wherever the bombardment had done its work and smashed down the wire entanglements, our men found it easy to advance. Such Turks as remained in the trenches were dazed and demoralised by the shell fire, and were only too willing to surrender. But in some parts, especially on the left of the line, the guns had failed to cut down the barbed wire, and here our men were crumpled up by the deadly fire of rifle and machine-gun which was concentrated on them at this point.

It was a soul-stirring sight to watch, on this great stage, the alternate advance and retreat of our men, and the scuttle of the Turks along their communication trenches; the charge of the Zouaves, the hurried retirement of the Senegalese when they were met with a terrific fire from the Turks; the reforming of the line behind the friendly crest; the renewed pounding of the Turkish line by French and British guns; the charge once more of the Allied infantry into and through the Turkish curtain of fire until they were swallowed up in the smoke.

The heart palpitated with emotion, and one's imagination was gripped by the sight of these gallant fellows flinging themselves recklessly at the Turks.

At length human nature could do no more, and both British and French had to call a halt.

The result of the battle was that we gained some few hundred yards practically along the whole front except on the extreme left, but it was at a considerable cost in killed and wounded.

CHAPTER XIV. GENERAL D'AMADE AND THE CORPS EXPÉDITIONNAIRE D'ORIENT

One end of our camp was in touch with the French lines and, of course, I saw a great deal of the French soldiers and a little of their gallant Commander, General d'Amade. I know, therefore, with what feelings of regret his men heard that he was about to return to France. He had endeared himself by his unfailing courtesy and goodwill, and had impressed with his fine, soldierly qualities all those with whom he had in any way come into contact.

During the tenure of his command, the French troops had, at the point of the bayonet, wrested seemingly impregnable positions from the brave foe. Their losses had been cruel, terrible, but their deeds are imperishable.

The military records of France make glorious reading, but even to these dazzling pages General d'Amade and his gallant troops have added fresh lustre.

A sad blow had fallen upon the General while he was in Alexandria reorganising his Corps Expéditionnaire d'Orient, prior to its departure for Gallipoli. In the midst of his work a telegram was handed to him announcing that his son had fallen gloriously in France. The General, having read the heart-breaking message, paused for a moment and then remarked: "Well, our work for France must go on."

It was my good fortune to see the order of the day of the *Journal Officiel* du 11 Février, 1915, which recounted the death and gallant deeds of General d'Amade's boy. He was only eighteen and had just joined his regiment, the 131st Infantry, when he went on a perilous night mission to obtain information which could only be got by creeping up into the German trenches. With just two men he accomplished this dangerous duty successfully, but at that very moment he was discovered and a volley from the enemy laid him low. Although grievously wounded, his first thought was for France, so, forbidding his comrades to carry him off, he told them to fly with all speed to the French lines with the valuable information which he had obtained. Young Gerard d'Amade died where he had fallen, a noble example of that spirit of self-sacrifice which characterises all ranks of the French Army.

A framed copy of this order of the day has now a place of honour in the nursery of a little boy I know of who, every night before he goes to bed, stands in front of it at the salute and says: "I do this in memory of a brave French officer who gave his life for his country. May I so live that, if necessary, I may be ready to die for England as nobly as Gerard d'Amade died for France."

The British public is little aware of what it owes to General d'Amade. During the terrible retreat of our Expeditionary Force from Mons, when we were outnumbered by five to one, and when the Germans were closing round our small army in overwhelming numbers, General Sir John French sent out urgent appeals for assistance in this hour of dire peril to the Generals commanding the French armies on his right and left. For some reason or other none of these came to his aid, and for a time it looked as if our gallant little army would be engulfed and annihilated.

Fortunately, there was one French General to whom the appeal was not made in vain. This was General d'Amade, who, at that time, was guarding the line in the northwest of France from Dunkerque to Valenciennes. To hold this very important eighty miles of front all the troops he had were four divisions of somewhat ill-equipped Territorials, with very few guns. It must be remembered that the French Territorial is past his prime and, as a rule, is the father of a family, and considers his fighting days over.

It can well be imagined, therefore, what an anxious time General d'Amade had during those fateful days from the 19th to the 28th August, 1914, when at any moment the German avalanche might burst upon him. On the 24th August his force was strengthened by two Reserve Divisions (the 61st and 62nd), which only arrived in the nick of time, for with these he was able to do something in answer to General French's despairing appeal. General d'Amade manoeuvred these two Reserve Divisions into a position which seriously threatened von Kluck's flank. That "hacking" General, not knowing the strength of General d'Amade's menacing force, became anxious for his right flank and communications, so turned aside from his pursuit of the British and proceeded to crush the French. These two divisions put up such an heroic fight and offered such a stubborn resistance to the German horde that it took the pressure off our sorely stricken men, enabling them to extricate themselves and retire, broken, exhausted, tired, crushed, it is true, but still to retire to safety, where they were able to reorganise and take ample vengeance on the Germans a few days later.

General d'Amade lost practically his entire force, but he had gained something very precious; he had saved our army from destruction, and what is more, he had saved the honour of France—nay, even France itself, for if the French generals had stood idly by and allowed our Expeditionary Force to be wiped out of existence, I think it is more than likely that France might have prayed in vain for any further assistance, in troops at all events, from England.

All honour, therefore, to the General who, without hesitation, with just two Reserve Divisions, took the shock of the German legions and sacrificed himself and his troops rather than see the honour of France go down in the dust. Politicians may recommend the bestowal of honours and decorations on their favourite Generals, but General d'Amade deserves more than this, he deserves a tribute from the British people. He made a magnificent sacrifice in our cause, and if ever in the history of the world a general deserved a sword of honour from a nation, General d'Amade deserves one from England.

CHAPTER XV. VARIOUS BOMBARDMENTS

Every morning regularly the Turks commenced shelling us punctually at eight o'clock, presumably after they had had breakfast, and again at tea time. They generally continued for a couple of hours, and these hours were always lively ones for us, and it was a daily occurrence to lose men, horses and mules.

On the 16th May, eleven Frenchmen, who happened to be close to our lines, were killed instantly by one shell, on the 17th one of my horses was wounded, and on the 19th the second was hit in the ribs by shrapnel.

The Turks often switched off from us and bombarded a section of the road used by wagons, gun-teams and motor cyclists. The latter were, to me, the chief wonder of Gallipoli. I ride a motor cycle myself, and have had a few smashes, so can fully realise its dangers.

I was introduced to this convenient form of locomotion by Dr. Rolleston after a breakdown in health. It is the most wonderful tonic I have yet come across, because the moment one gets on to the bicycle one's attention is so centred on keeping it going, picking out the smoothest bits of road, avoiding collisions, etc., that I veritably believe the treachery of one's closest friend would, for the moment, at least, fade from the memory. I am perfectly certain that the Gallipoli motor cyclists never gave a thought to absent friends; they were much too busy avoiding pitfalls and shells. They flew over the most uneven ground, took small trenches as it were in their stride, and were generally the most dare-devil set of boys I have ever seen. Many a time we stood and watched through our glasses this dangerous strip of road which the Turks had got the range of to a yard. As the wagons, gun-teams and cyclists approached it, they would get up the pace, and fly through it at top speed. The narrow squeaks that we constantly witnessed on this bit of road were enough to make one's hair stand on end! Yet I am glad to say I only once saw a man struck down. It looked so sad—the moment before so full of the joy of life, and then, just a little, huddled heap, lying still and quiet on the dusty roadway.

On May 20th, the Turks bombarded us for several hours; five of my men were wounded, two seriously, one of the poor fellows having his leg smashed to atoms. The same day I had five mules and one horse killed and ten mules wounded. The Horse Artillery, camped round about us, also suffered rather severely, for the Turks every now and again switched their batteries on to their lines and caused them heavy losses. It was a busy time for Lieutenant Fisher, the Veterinary Surgeon of the Horse Batteries, who kindly came to our aid whenever the Zion mules got "strafed."

When this bombardment broke upon us, everybody made a rush to get his horse, mule or himself out of danger, and many were the curses heaped on the Turkish gunners, who were universally consigned to the warmest place of which we have ever heard. It makes me laugh even now when I think of a little comedy that took place between Rolo and his groom. The latter, whose name was Dabani, was a most comical looking little fellow, with bandy legs, a swarthy face, and little black beard sprouting in patches here and there. He was an Israelite from Arabia, and although an excellent fellow in many ways, he was more renowned for his piety than for his courage. You could always tell the intensity of a bombardment by the fervour of Dabani's prayers. On this occasion, when the shells began to burst and spatter the shrapnel all round us, Rolo shouted to Dabani, whom he saw scuttling off for safety, to come back and look after his horse. "What, look after your horse now?" cried Dabani. "This is a time when I must look after myself," and taking not the slightest notice of Rolo's angry maledictions, he, with rabbit-like agility, dived for safety into his dug-out!

This bombardment badly shook some of my men, and among them Schoub, my farrier, who, the moment he felt it safe to emerge from the nethermost depths of his dug-out, came in a state of abject terror to Gye, begging piteously to be sent back to the bosom of his family in Alexandria, because, he remarked, "I am no use here now. The shells have made me stone deaf. I cannot hear a word." "What," said Gye, in a low voice, "not a single word?" "Not a single word," replied Schoub!

It was many months before he returned in safety to Alexandria, and by that time bombardments had become so common that they had ceased to terrify.

On the 2nd June, I was returning with Claude Rolo from an expedition which we had made to the Gurkha trenches on the extreme left of the line. Before we had got very far on our way heavy howitzers began to bombard the Turks, and as we were just then passing an artillery observation post, hidden away in a cross trench, we turned aside and went into it. From here we could see our high explosive shells bursting with terrific effect on the Turkish trench, which was only about three hundred yards away. The Artillery Observation Officer telephoned back to the guns the result of each shot, and under his guidance the shells soon battered down the earthworks, pulverising everything where they fell. Soon, however, some sharp-eyed Turkish gunner spotted our observation post and began to plug at us pretty rapidly. Shells hopped off the parapet, shrapnel struck the steel shield, fuses and fragments of all kinds thudded into the bank behind our backs, and we seemed for the moment to be living in a little tornado of lead and iron. When this had continued for a few minutes, I remarked to the gunner man: "What on earth are the Turks trying to hit?" "Hit us, of course," he somewhat shortly replied.

Now, so long as we remained here in the deep trench we were comparatively safe, but as I wanted to get back to camp, I thought I would pull the gunner's leg before leaving him; he had no idea who we were, for we were in our shirt sleeves as usual, so I pretended to be thoroughly scared, and said: "Good heavens, this is no place for me!" on which he smiled the smile of a brave man who feels pity for a poltroon. There were some twenty yards or so of open ground to be covered the moment we left the shelter of the observation post, and, of course, this was a really dangerous strip, because it was exposed to the fire of the Turks, and had therefore to be covered at top speed. The only way of accomplishing this in safety was to do it in between the shells, and as there was only a couple of seconds between each, the plunge out had to be made the instant one burst, so as to be under cover before the next arrived. Warning Rolo to follow me after the next explosion, out we darted. We had almost reached safety when I heard coming after us the scream of an approaching shell. I shouted out to Rolo, "Jump for your life!" and at the same time threw myself down, and the last thing I saw, amid the dust kicked up by the shower of shrapnel bullets, was Rolo plunging head foremost into a ditch, as if he were taking a dive!

We were neither of us hurt, but a stone thrown up by the shell struck me on the hand and drew a little blood. We both congratulated ourselves on our lucky escape and got back to camp with whole skins, none the worse for our close shave.

CHAPTER XVI. THE COMING OF THE GERMAN SUBMARINES

In our nightly journeys back from the trenches we were always guided through the darkness to our camp by the brilliant glare of the lights from the warships, hospital ships and transports, which lay thickly clustered round Cape Helles. It was a most beautiful sight, like a veritable floating Venice, but it was not practical and it was not war. It showed an arrogance and utter contempt of the enemy who was, at that very moment, stealthily stalking them under the seas with the deadly submarine.

At all events, the submarines came, with the result that the battleships *Goliath* and *Triumph* were sunk with appalling swiftness and great loss of life.

Then, and then only, did the Fleet awaken to its danger; the battleships and cruisers vanished into the unknown, while the transports disappeared in a night, and we felt, as it were, marooned on this inhospitable Peninsula, from which the Turks had removed every living thing, save only a few dogs, which were found to be so dangerous that they had to be shot at sight.

It was, therefore, with feelings of great pleasure that, as I rode down to W Beach on the evening of the 26th May, I saw the stately battleship, the *Majestic*, lying at anchor out in the roadstead, a few cable lengths from W Beach; and as I looked my heart grew glad within me, because there lay the ship in the open sea, exposed to any attack, and I felt that it would be impossible for the ship to lie thus unless the German submarines which had sunk the other battleships a few days previously were either disposed of, or else some clever new defence had been designed which made the *Majestic* immune from the deadly torpedo.

It was a cheering thought, and it helped to enhance the beauty of the wondrous panorama which lay spread before my eyes.

Away to my left stood the quaint old ruined walls and towers of Sedd-el-Bahr, thrown into bold outline against the rippling waters of the Dardanelles, while further on the eye was caught by the green plains of Ilium, set in a tangle of hills, on the picturesque Asiatic coast. Ahead of me, to the south, glittered the soft sea, with Cape Helles jutting into it, like a rough brown hand thrust into a basin of shimmering quicksilver. Almost at my feet lay Lancashire Landing, busy with its hundreds of men and animals going to and fro, while away on my right sparkled the Ægean, with the Isles of Greece jutting out of it, like rugged giants rising from their ocean lair. To crown all, the sun was going down in a perfect blaze of colour, tipping the crests of Imbros and Samothrace with a glint of gold, as it sank behind them into the sea. I have seen sunsets in many parts of the world, but never have I seen anything to equal the glorious lights and shades which at sundown are painted on the Ægean sky. If I were an artist, my ambition would be to go in the lovely autumn days on a pilgrimage to these shores and humbly try to put on my canvas the perfectly gorgeous but harmoniously blended rose, pink, scarlet, red, yellow, purple, green, amber and blue— a perfect intoxication of glorious colours which the imagination would be unequal to, unless they were absolutely thrown on the sky before one's own eyes. The magnificence of the sunsets seen from Gallipoli were the sum of what an ordinary mortal could conceive as a fitting setting for the splendour of God's Throne.

So it is to be hoped that the officers and crew of the *Majestic*, which was moored so peacefully amid such heavenly surroundings, took a soul-satisfying view of the glory around them, because, alas, for many of the poor fellows it was the last sunset that would ever gladden their eyes, for on the morning of the 27th the ship was marked down by a German submarine and sent to its doom within four minutes of being struck.

I was attending to some routine work in my camp when I heard the terrific explosion and, looking up, saw a volume of smoke ascending to the heavens from W Beach. I jumped on my horse, which was ready saddled close by, and galloped over to hear what had happened. When I topped the rise, all of the *Majestic* that I could see was a couple of dozen feet of its copper keel which projected above the water, and which still remains thus—a mute witness to the fact that "some one had blundered."

Regrettable incidents like these should be unknown in a Navy renowned for the good practical commonsense and thoroughness of its captains.

CHAPTER XVII. TRENCH WARFARE IN GALLIPOLI

"From all forms of trench warfare, preserve us, O Lord!" should be the humble prayer of every soldier, for it is about the most unpleasant, tiresome, humdrum, disagreeable, dangerous, death-without-glory kind of warfare which the evil genius of man could devise. As, however, it has come to stay, it may perhaps be of interest to describe what it was like in Gallipoli.

When, after the first battles, the Turks refused any longer to meet us in the open, and took to the trenches, which they had, with great energy, dug right across the Peninsula, it became necessary for us to adopt the same mole-like tactics, and our advance was brought practically to a standstill. Instead of going ahead a couple of miles in a day's fight, it now became a question of taking one trench at a time, and often we did not gain as much as that, even after the most strenuous battles.

Long lines of trenches, from three to six or more feet deep, and three or four feet wide, were dug in zig-zags right across the Peninsula, more or less parallel to the Turkish lines, and behind these were similar support and reserve trenches; at the back of these again were second and third line defence trenches; while still further were the so-called rest trenches, but in Gallipoli these were just as dangerous as the front trenches, owing to the confined space in which the army was cooped up, and also owing to the configuration of the ground, which exposed them to fire from Achi Baba as well as from the guns in Asia. Some of our trenches were so deep that hundreds of scaling ladders were always kept in readiness to enable the men to swarm out quickly when an assault was to be made. Long lines of communication trenches ran up and down and to and fro, connecting the various lines of trenches, and many of these were dug deep enough and wide enough to give ample cover for mules and horses. Various little back alleys were also dug in different directions, so that the whole face of the country was transformed into a veritable rabbit warren. These communication trenches were necessary so that reliefs, reinforcements, munitions, food and water could be taken up in safety to the firing line.

Where the ground was very hard and deep trenches could not be dug, the necessary cover was given by building parapets made of sandbags, little canvas bags about two feet long and ten inches across, which could easily be carried by one man when filled with sand or clay. These sandbags should be of different colours, because otherwise when one is taken out to make a loophole the blank space is seen at once and the enemy's fire is concentrated on it. In Gallipoli our sandbags were all of the same colour—drab-coloured canvas.

When an attack was made and an enemy's trench was captured, thousands of these sandbags were carried forward, and by piling them up a new protective trench was rapidly constructed, for, of course, the original Turkish trench was always battered to pieces (or should have been) by high explosive shells before the attack was launched.

Another great use of the sandbag was to erect a barrier across an enemy communication trench, otherwise, of course, he could pour his troops down the communication alley and perhaps effect a surprise. It was exceedingly odd to see our sentry on one side of such a barrier and the Turkish sentry on the other side, apparently quite friendly in the intervals of bombing each other!

One day a man of the Inniskilling Fusiliers played a trick on the Turkish sentry. Finding life rather monotonous, and being somewhat fed up with bully beef, he bored a hole in his tin, stuck a cartridge into it, and hurled the novel projectile over the sandbag barrier among the Turks, who could be heard flying for their lives away from it along the trench, evidently thinking it was some new form of diabolical bomb we had invented. Then one man, a little bolder than the rest, could be heard cautiously stalking it; he even threw stones at it, and when these failed to cause an explosion, he plucked up enough courage to hook it towards him with his fixed bayonet. It was apparently sent off for investigation to some German professor in the rear, for some few hours later the Turkish sentry shouted out loudly over the parapet: "Bully beef, bully beef; throw us more," and this little incident led to many friendly exchanges of bully or cigarettes.

Life in the trenches when no "strafe" was on was very monotonous—dull, weary watching and waiting, with dust blowing into one's eyes and mouth and nose all the time, and flies everywhere. While in the trenches food had to be snatched when it was possible to get it. It was cooked some considerable distance to the rear and was then carried up to the trenches in great pots and there distributed, and in Gallipoli, of course, that meant dividing it between men and flies—the latter getting the lion's share during the months of June, July and August.

Of course, work was always going on. The trenches had to be carefully drained and sloped so as to allow the rainfall to flow off. If this were not properly done they would inevitably be flooded out in the rains, and life in them would be impossible. Even when every care was taken they sometimes became raging torrents. Much ground was made good by digging out from the trenches towards the Turkish lines and forming a fresh line of trenches closer to the enemy and in a better position.

Every yard in front of the trenches was guarded by barbed wire, sometimes left unrolled on the ground, where it naturally goes into coils and traps for the unwary, and sometimes interlaced on stakes, like a regular wire fencing, doubled many times. It was very dangerous work putting up this form of defence, and it was generally done at night, but even then the enemy could see our men by the light of the brilliant flares which were constantly sent up, for these remained in the air for several seconds, making everything as bright as day. The only chance of escape then was to lie flat down and remain perfectly still until the flare went out.

Then there was the constant arduous and dangerous labour of sapping, i. e., tunnelling underground from our trenches underneath the Turkish trenches, making a huge cavity there, filling it with explosives and blowing the trench and such Turks as were in it sky high. This was generally done when an attack was made, so as to throw the enemy into greater confusion.

At night it was usual to man the front trenches fairly strongly, one-third of the force always being awake and on the look-out for the enemy.

Of course, it was almost certain death for a man to stand up and show his head and shoulders above the parapet line, so the watch on the enemy was kept by men with periscopes, who could see every move in perfect safety. Even the periscopes were often shattered to pieces by the bullets of the Turks, which shows that some of them were good marksmen.

Telephone wires were laid everywhere in the trenches, and telephone operators and observing officers were scattered up and down the line. On the first sign of an enemy attack these officers communicated with their Batteries in the rear, and within two seconds a curtain of fire was rained on the advancing foe, which, in most cases, he found it quite impossible to get through. If he ever succeeded, however, the Infantry were by this time lining the parapets, ready to mow down the enemy with rifle and machine-gun fire, so the only marvel is that any of the assaulting force ever got through. A very rare occurrence—and those that did pierce the line never again got back to their own trenches.

One day I went up to visit Lieutenant Davidson, who was Forward Observing Officer, and he, having occasion to fire a gun, telephoned to the Battery; it was a distinctly weird feeling to hear the scream of the shell from the guns two miles back flying close over our heads into the Turkish trenches in front of us, almost before Davidson had ceased speaking! At that same observation post, on a previous day, another R. H. A. officer, Lieutenant Perceval, who also was a member of our little mess, had a very narrow escape. A Turkish shell came through, slightly bruised his shoulder, and killed his Bombardier, who was, at the moment, holding the telephone.

In the side of the trench next the enemy little niches were excavated where men could lie and sit fairly well sheltered from wind and rain. These recesses were often used by the Turks as burial places for their dead. I remember on one occasion I was walking along a piece of the line which we had just taken from the Turks when a shell exploded close to the trench. The concussion shook away some loose earth and out from the side of the trench popped a dead hand and arm!—just as if a policeman had put out his hand to stop the traffic. The dead Turk seemed to try, even in death, to bar the way to an enemy's approach.

A very disagreeable feature of trench life is the unpleasant odour of the dead, which penetrates everywhere, for, of course, when an attack is made by one side or the other hundreds may be killed close to the trenches, and as a rule it is impossible either to rescue the wounded or to bury the dead, because the enemy would inevitably shoot down any one attempting such a task.

One of the very worst trials of trench warfare is to see the dead body of a comrade lying out in the open, gradually fading away before one's eyes, a mummied hand still clutching the rifle, the helmet a little way off, looking ever so weird in its gruesome surroundings.

While in the trenches one is, of course, subject at all times to shells, rifle fire, mine explosions, poison gas, bombs, liquid fire, and other diabolical inventions. The Turks, however, did not use either poison gas or liquid fire, and, of course, neither did the British.

Worst trial of all is the trench mortar! This venomous weapon sends a bomb weighing a hundred pounds or more of the most deadly high explosive plumb into the midst of a trench with marvellous accuracy at any range up to four hundred yards. The vicious thing can be seen soaring high up into the air, until it reaches a point directly overhead, then it hovers for a moment, like a hawk over its prey, and finally swoops down, pulverising everybody and everything near which it explodes.

From my own observation of trench warfare I would say unhesitatingly that no assault should be launched against the enemy until his trenches had been thoroughly pounded to pieces by high explosive, his men demoralised by a constant stream of shells, and all wire entanglements or other barriers swept out of the way of the advance. Then, and then only, should the infantry attack be launched, but before doing so the supports and reserves should be brought up as close as possible to the firing line, because, in these days especially, the speed with which an assault can be reinforced makes all the difference between victory and defeat.

During the assault the guns should be constantly playing on the reserve trenches of the enemy, the counter batteries (i. e., those batteries told off to dominate enemy batteries) firing as fast as they possibly can to keep down enemy shrapnel fire and generally supporting the attack in every possible way. Special groups should always be told off (not single individuals) with orders to signal back to the batteries the position which the front line has reached in the assault, otherwise—and I have seen it happen more than once—our own guns will be found playing on our own men.

It is unwise to trust to telephone wires for passing signals back to the batteries, for they are often cut by shells or broken by passing troops. Aeroplanes fitted with wireless are most useful. Another good plan is to fasten some very conspicuous object, such as a large tin disc, to the backs of the men, so that the gunners would always be able to tell at whom they were firing. The disc should be tied so that the men could switch it round to the front if they were forced to retire. This plan was adopted in Gallipoli towards the end of July with excellent results, for our men could always be made out by the flashing of the tin, which, of course, the enemy could not see.

Bombs should always be carried with the assaulting columns, and the bomb throwers should not be hampered by a rifle, but should only be armed with revolver and bayonet, for when their stock of bombs is expended there are always plenty of rifles lying around belonging to the dead and badly wounded.

When all these arrangements have been completed, and a combined attack is made with shells, machine-guns, rifle fire, trench mortars, poison gas, liquid fire, etc., the attack is almost certain to succeed at some point or other, and once the defender's line is broken his whole line is threatened, and if the reserves are brought up and poured quickly enough into the breach, so as to get a wedge in between the enemy's forces, his army can then be smashed up in detail and a great victory won.

Cavalry can then burst through and once more come into their own by playing havoc with the enemy's line of communication. Of course, in Gallipoli we had no Cavalry; at least, such mounted men as we had came as Infantry without horses! and I must say that they fought well, those yeomen from Bucks and Kent—the only pity is that we did not have more of them. When we did make a breach in the enemy's line, we never had enough troops to push through and so ensure a crushing victory.

CHAPTER XVIII. GUNS AND STAFF

The losses which we suffered in every attack on the Turkish trenches were very severe, and it was painful to see our men frittered away time after time in these hopeless assaults on what had now become an impregnable position—impregnable at all events to such forces as we could launch to the attack. Our casualties at the original landing had reduced the 29th Division to a mere skeleton. Many of the Battalions were not a company strong and had scarcely any officers left, and it was found necessary to join the remnants of two or three together to make one rather weak Battalion. The Dublins and Munsters were thus linked up together and were officially known as the "Dubsters."

Reinforcements only came in by driblets, and as they came they were eaten up in futile attacks on the strong trenches which the Turks had meanwhile, with great energy, dug right across the Peninsula.

We were never really strong enough to undertake a serious offensive, and our guns never had ammunition enough to prepare the way properly by a devastating bombardment. Half an hour or an hour was usually about all we were able to do in the way of knocking the Turkish trenches about with high explosive, whereas these same trenches needed a steady rain of shells for several days to crumple them up and destroy the scores of machine-guns which bristled everywhere. Trench warfare seemed to have taken us completely by surprise; we were without trench mortars, but luckily were able to borrow some from the French; neither had we any bombs or hand grenades, except such as we could manufacture locally out of jam tins!

No battery commander was allowed to fire a single round unless he had first obtained permission from his Brigadier, and even when a couple of battalions of Turkish troops well within range could be observed marching in column, the Brigadier was compelled to limit the battery to two rounds only, for to such dire straits were we reduced owing to lack of ammunition!

Even with the slight support given by the guns I have seen our gallant fellows time after time leap out of their trenches and, in an irresistible onslaught with the bayonet, sweep over trench upon trench full of Turkish soldiers. Nowhere could the enemy stand up to our men in the open, as was proved over and over again in the early days of the fight before they took to trench warfare. If only we had had enough ammunition and one more Division, equal to the 29th, we would have retrieved the initial mistake of landing at Helles, and have swept the Turks over Achi Baba from their positions round the Narrows, and Constantinople itself would have been in our grip within a month.

But, alas! we hadn't the ammunition and we hadn't the men; and when the Turks took to mole tactics, and protected their front with those two inventions of the Evil One—barbed wire and machine-guns—our case, considering the means at our disposal, was a hopeless one.

During a fierce battle which took place in June, I was standing close to one of our batteries in position, just south of the Pink Farm, and what a contrast it was to see these guns in action after having repeatedly watched the French .75s! Here was no smooth barrel-recoil, but a clumsy spade stuck in the ground to prevent the piece from kicking. Whenever the gun was fired it jumped back like a bucking bronco, necessitating the relaying of the gun after each shot.

We have better guns than that now, of course, but with all our mechanical superiority and mechanical resources we should years ago have had a gun equal, or superior, to the French .75. Of course there is no use in having a quick-firing gun if you cannot have mountains of ammunition alongside of it, and this point should never be lost sight of by the Staff, whose duty it is to look after such matters.

As we were very short of high explosive shells the battery was not doing a great deal of firing, and in the lull a Staff Officer rode up and told the Battery Commander to lay his guns on to some Turks whom he pointed out, saying they were threatening our line.

Now I had been watching this part of the battlefield most carefully through my glasses, and I had seen our own men advance and go into the position which the Staff Officer said was held by the Turks. I overheard his instructions to the gunner officer, so I called out: "Those are our men, not Turks!" However, in spite of my warning, a couple of rounds were loosed off, and they were only too well placed, for they exploded among our unfortunate troops, doing, no doubt, a considerable amount of damage, because, in a moment, a wrathful telephone message came to the Battery Commander telling him to cease fire instantly, on which the discreet Staff Officer made a hurried departure.

While we had some excellent Staff Officers, there were others not exactly noted for their brilliancy, and no doubt the Turks saw that some of our "regrettable incidents" were due to bad Staff work, and the following story was vouched for by the Peninsula wag.

It had been noted with some surprise that, though the Turkish sniper exacted his toll from all other ranks, the Staff appeared to be immune. At last the mystery was solved when one of these sharpshooters was captured, for on being asked how it was that the Staff always escaped, he replied: "Oh, well, you see, I get five shillings for every private I shoot, ten shillings for every sergeant, a pound for every officer, but if I were to shoot a Staff Officer I would be shot myself!"

I need hardly say that these merry quips made at the expense of the Staff by our frolicsome wits should be taken with a grain of salt. So far as my own experience goes, the Staff Officers of the 29th Division, and, later, of the 8th Army Corps, were all that could be desired, and at them no such gibe could be levelled. All those with whom I came in contact were very much all there at their respective jobs.

There is no doubt, however, that there is some reason for the general lack of confidence in the Staff. Responsible positions are unfortunately too often given to most unsuitable men, with regrettable results.

Glaring instances of jobbery and favouritism are so universally known that it is unnecessary to quote examples. Puck must be having the time of his life. If only our responsible administrators would for the future abjure nepotism (vain wish!) and give proved talent a chance, we should, I am convinced, have something better to show than "strategic retreats" and "brilliant evacuations."

I am reminded of an incident that occurred when I was staying with Colonel Roosevelt during the time he was President of the United States. An influential and well-known Senator came into the room while I was there, and urged on the President the claims of a *protégé* of his to a post as Mining Inspector. President Roosevelt's reply impressed me very much: "Well, Senator, if your man is the best Mining Engineer that can be found in the United States he shall get the job, but not otherwise; he will have the lives of men in his hands."

Mark this, ye jobbites of England!

CHAPTER XIX. VISITS TO THE TRENCHES

During one of the hot June days Gye and I paid a visit to Colonel Bruce and his Gurkhas, who were holding the left of the line down by the Ægean Sea.

The Gurkhas have done some splendid work in the Peninsula. They are in their element when out at night doing reconnoitring work. Bruce told me of the valuable report brought in by one of his N. C. O.'s, on the strength of which he took his men up the side of a cliff and was able to surprise and drive the Turks out of a very strong position which it was of prime importance we should hold. Other troops had several times attempted this feat, but failed because they attacked in the open, while the Gurkhas succeeded owing to good reconnoitring work.

The night previous to our visit the Turks had made a most determined attack on the Gurkhas, and the Gurkhas asked for no better sport. Flares, shot up by our officers, showed the Turks advancing in regular parade formation in line of columns. As soon as the Turks saw that they had been observed, they charged, yelling their war cry: "Allah, Allah!" The Gurkhas waited patiently, lining the trenches as thickly as they could stand. They allowed the Turks to approach within about fifty yards of them and then opened such a hurricane of rifle and machine-gun fire that the Turks were absolutely crumpled up in ranks as they stood. The fury of the Gurkhas was now thoroughly aroused and, the reserves having been brought up, the whole brigade made such an onslaught that practically not a single Turk out of that huge attacking force ever got back to his own trench.

When Rolo and I viewed the battlefield within a few hours of the fight, there were still some wounded to be seen in the intervening ground between the two forces, while in regular battle array lay line upon line of Turkish dead, silent witnesses to the terribly accurate fire poured into them by the Gurkhas. They are brave fellows, those Turks, and it was a sad sight to see so many gallant men laid low.

No doubt in revenge for the defeat they had suffered the previous night, the Turks were bombarding the Gurkha lines vigorously, and while I was there they landed a big "Black Maria" shell underneath a little fellow who was squatting on his heels outside his dug-out. It was an extraordinary sight to see him shoot down the hill in this position and land some forty feet away in a clump of bushes, from which he emerged not much the worse for his involuntary flight.

The Gurkhas, in one of their previous attacks on the heights occupied by the Turks, were held up by some barbed wire and had to retire. A private soldier, however, chose to remain behind, ensconced under the scanty protection of a couple of knapsacks, which he pulled together from those strewn round, thinking that he could hold his own until another assault was delivered by his comrades, when he would join them. No comrades came, however, so he found himself unable to move without being observed. He therefore pretended to be dead and lay absolutely still for hours, not even daring to move his head, except when his neck got very stiff, and then only by pushing his hat up a fraction of an inch, so that he might slowly twist his head inside it without showing any movement. At last he could stand the strain no longer, so he leaped up, raced in a zig-zag to his own trenches amid a hail of bullets, and, carefully avoiding a low spot where the Turks had concentrated their fire, expecting him to go in that way, he leaped over the highest part of the parapet and escaped scot-free.

I saw this little fellow a few hours after his exploit and he looked as though he had thoroughly enjoyed the adventure.

A few days after the big Turkish assault I was again on my way to this part of the line, when I happened to meet General de Lisle, and, on mentioning that I was going to see Colonel Bruce, he told me I would not find him, for he had been wounded on the previous night by a bomb, while gallantly leading his men.

I had several friends in the Inniskilling Fusiliers and frequently I came across them in my journeys to and from the Gurkha lines. As a rule, they held the trenches to the right of the little brown men from Nepaul.

I always made a point, when I was anywhere near, of looking up Captain Gordon Tillie. He was now practically the only officer left of the Inniskillings who had taken part in the original landing and had, so far, escaped scot-free. I was hopeful that his luck would see him through, because he had only been married a few days before he left England for the front, and I knew his wife very well, and had promised her to look him up whenever I had an opportunity.

Just before the 29th Division went to Suvla, Gye and I paid him a visit, while he was holding the front trenches, and, sad to say, this was the last occasion on which I ever saw Gordon Tillie. He took us along that portion of the trench for which his company was responsible, and showed us the various points of interest in the Turkish line, which, at this particular place, was sometimes parallel, and sometimes almost at right angles to our trenches, and in places only a dozen yards distant. When I was leaving him he cautioned me to be careful of a certain part of the trench we should have to pass through, as he said it was exposed to the Turkish guns and they often gave it a "strafing." My parting remark to him was: "Take care they don't 'strafe' you."

Of course, shells were dropping here and there all the time from the Turkish guns, and they were paying some attention to the piece of dangerous trench which Gye and I were bound to go through, so, saying to him: "Let's make a bolt for it," we started off at our best pace, but before we got through we had to lie down in the bottom of the trench to escape a couple of shells which burst all round us and knocked to pieces the sandbag parapet protecting our heads.

Gordon Tillie's friendly warning may have saved our lives, and it is a nice thought, for, soon afterwards, the 29th Division were sent to Suvla, and there Captain Tillie was killed while gallantly leading his company up the slopes of Sari Bair—a brave soldier, as Sir Ian Hamilton testifies in his Suvla Bay Despatch.

I often made an expedition to visit a friend, only to find, when I got there, that he had perhaps been killed the day before, or else had been sent off to hospital badly wounded, and it was sad to see how one's friends gradually got thinned off. Many of them lay buried all round. One would suddenly be startled by coming across a freshly-dug grave in some sheltered little nook by the wayside and learn for the first time, from the rude cross erected over it, that one's friend lay there. But war is war, and as a shell or bullet may come at any moment and bring sudden death with it to one's self, one gets used to the idea, and somehow it does not seem so dreadful. Many of us often escaped by the merest chance. In my own case the turning aside to pluck a flower, or straying a little from the path to get a better view of a sunset, was the chance that prevented Death from finding me, because more than once I have seen a shell explode and excavate a huge hole on the exact spot where, had I not turned aside, I would undoubtedly have been standing. Yes, indeed, in those days, one often heard, sounding softly in one's ears, the faint rustle of the wings of the Angel of Death.

I do not know whether the Turks had any particular spite against my Zionists, but they certainly gave us more than our fair share of shells. One afternoon they began a bombardment and plumped a shell into a bank on which sat a Zion man, Private Scorobogaty. The explosion sent him some feet into the air, but, beyond the bruise and shock, he suffered no damage. The next shell dropped plump in the middle of our little supply of stores, within six feet of the door of our dug-out, and sent everything flying through space. A third shot plunged into the roots of a tree which stood close to our lines, by which the trumpeter of L Battery, R. H. A., was standing. He heard the shell coming, and, without any particular reason, but luckily for him, he made a dive to the right instead of to the left, and so escaped for the moment. Next afternoon at tea-time another shell came, cut the same tree clean in two, wounding the trumpeter and two other men of L Battery, who were having their tea in its shade.

CHAPTER XX. FLIES, DUST AND BATTLE

July was a scorching month, and to add to the discomfort of heat there was a plague of flies; flies, flies, flies everywhere, and I have no doubt that they were responsible for the serious epidemics which broke out among the troops. Doubtless it was the self-same pestilence which Homer tells us attacked the Grecian Army camped round Troy, and which they attributed to the anger of Apollo, though none of our mules suffered as did those of the Greeks.

These flies were disgusting, horrible pests, for they would come straight from the rotting corpses of the Turks, which lay in unburied hundreds in front of our trenches, and blacken every scrap of food on which they could obtain a foot-hold. The only way to get a clean bite into one's mouth, without taking the flies with it, was to blow vigorously all the time until the lips had actually closed on the morsel, and even then these pests would hover round, waiting for a chance opening to dart in and chase it down.

The dust, too, in these days was very trying, for the whole peninsula was now one vast dust heap, which the slightest wind would swirl about in blinding, choking clouds. I noticed that on several occasions our men had to do battle with this dust storm blowing directly in their eyes, so that it was impossible to see anything in front of them, while the Turks, with their backs to it, could see our men coming along plainly enough and could slate them at their leisure. I always found, as was to be expected, that when we foolishly attacked on such days as these we effected nothing beyond getting ourselves killed. The Turks must have marvelled at our blind folly.

I well remember that one of our most successful battles was fought on a day when the wind carried the dust into the faces of the Turks; towards the close of this fight I saw a couple of battalions go right through and over all the Turkish trenches within sight, and then get engulfed in a great ravine on the very slope of Achi Baba itself, where they were hidden from view, and then I saw thousands of Turks stream down through communication trenches on each side of our men, filling the trenches in their rear, as could be plainly seen by the bristling bayonets which showed above the parapets.

I felt that these two battalions were lost, as indeed they were for two or three days, but somehow or other, after some extraordinary hide-and-seek experiences among the Turkish trenches, they fought their way back again, clearing the Turks out of their path, in hand-to-hand fighting, as they hacked their way back to our own lines.

A friend of mine, Captain Braham of the 6th Manchesters, had a narrow escape on one occasion when he made an attempt to lead his men in an assault. Being short of ammunition for the guns, the Turkish trenches had not been properly bombarded; Turkish machine-guns and riflemen were still in position, ready to mow our men down the moment they leaped from their trenches. This was the fate which overtook the 6th Manchesters; they were practically cut to pieces before they had advanced more than a dozen yards from their lines, and the few survivors thought it wiser to get back to cover as quickly as possible. Captain Braham, however, tried to rally them out of the trench again, and at that moment, while standing on the parapet, a bullet struck his knapsack, cut through the buckle, a box of chocolate and a tin-opener. The tin-opener diverted the bullet out through the bottom of the haversack by his heels, but the impact of it was so great that it knocked him off the parapet into the trench, as if he had been struck with a sledge hammer. He told me afterwards that he did not know at the time what had knocked him over, and it was not until he had removed his haversack that the mystery was explained.

During one of these dog days Rolo and I went as far forward as it was possible to go, so that we might get a close view of a battle which was to begin at 11 A. M. on the 12th of July.

Punctually to the minute our guns crashed out along the line and pounded away steadily for an hour. Then we watched the attack, and what impressed me in this battle, as it did also in others, was the inadequate force with which we attempted to take the offensive. A line of our men would dash forward, take two or three Turkish trenches, losing perhaps half its effective strength in so doing, and then find itself too weak to do more than hold on, and very often they could not even do that. There seemed to be no regular system of sending line after line at intervals into the fight. I know that this was arranged for in orders, but it did not always come off, and the men who had, with such gallantry and at such a cost, taken the trenches, would be forced out of them in a counter-attack by overwhelming numbers of Turks, and, in getting back to their own lines, would again lose heavily.

To obtain a view of the battlefield from a different point we made our way along a communication trench, and here our interest in the fight in the front was abruptly switched off and centred on ourselves, for the Turks had spotted a Battalion of Lancashire Fusiliers coming along to reinforce the firing line, and they turned a most deadly and accurate fire upon us from the Turkish guns. Shells hopped from the parapets or broke them in all round us, crashed over our heads, and even plumped right into the trench itself, sending men flying in all directions.

The Lancashire Fusiliers had, therefore, to halt and take cover under the lee of the parapet, and during this time one of the men asked Claude Rolo what his job was in these parts, for, being in our shirt-sleeves, and pretty grimy with dust and with climbing about the trenches, he could not make out who or what we were.

When Rolo replied: "Oh, I've only come to see the show," "Oh, Hell," said the Lancashire man, "you must be mad to come to a show like this on your own."

I felt very sorry for the poor lads when they finally marched off. The day was hot enough to make one feel that the only way to keep cool was to sit in one's bones under the shade of a tree, and yet here were these Lancashire men loaded down with the whole weight of their packs—food, ammunition, blanket, belts, bayonet and rifle—marching on through this infernal heat to a bloody combat, where they would have to put forth all their efforts in getting rapidly across the fire-swept ground, plunge into and out of deep trenches, and, in addition, grapple hand to hand with no mean foe.

Some things are more than human nature can stand. You cannot overload the soldier, and then expect him to pull his full weight in battle with the broiling sun burning out his throat.

The Lancashire lads were soon in the thick of the fight, and a great many never again needed the shelter of a friendly trench.

We lost a few prisoners to the Turks in this battle owing to exhaustion, and it is a comfort to know that our gallant enemies treat such men of ours as fall into their hands with kindness. I never heard anything but praise for the Turk and the way he played the game. I only knew of one case of a prisoner being mutilated, and this may have been the work of a German, for the victim was a Sikh, and died before any evidence could be taken. The Turk is a clean fighter, and more than once they have pointed out to us that they would be glad if we would move a hospital ship a little further from the transports, for they feared that in firing at the latter they might hit the hospital, and, so far as the records go, this is more than would have been done by the Germans.

Among the prisoners taken in one of these battles were some German sailors from the *Goeben*, who had been working the machine-guns. When taken they had no more ammunition left, their officer and many others had been killed, and their position was quite hopeless, so they gladly surrendered. They looked crestfallen and sullen when I saw them as prisoners on their way to the beach.

During these hot July days the Turkish shells would often set fire to the dried-up gorse and bracken near our lines, and, as the wind usually came from the north, I have seen a raging line of fire, hundreds of yards long, with flames forty feet high, roaring and crackling down to our trenches.

Our men, however, had taken the precaution of cutting gorse down in front, so that the fire never actually overwhelmed our lines.

The Turks did not lack initiative; their snipers gave us a considerable amount of trouble all the time we were on the Peninsula. Two of these men obtained some celebrity by their daring and originality. They actually concealed themselves between some of our guns, and before they were hunted down and shot they had killed and wounded several of our officers and men. They were painted green all over, face, hands, clothes, and even their rifles, while little green bushes, similar to the gorse around, were tied to their heads.

Their sense of humour showed itself in some rather quaint ways. Once, when a bomb was thrown over a barricade by a French soldier, hitting a Turk on the head without exploding, the latter shouted back "Assassin, Assassin!" On another occasion, on the completion of one of the heaviest bombardments to which we had subjected their trenches—a perfect storm of shells from field guns, siege guns, howitzers and battleships—as soon as the firing ceased and the dust cleared away, a huge placard was slowly raised from the front trench, on which was printed in large letters "No Casualties."

CHAPTER XXI. WORK OF THE ZION MULE CORPS

During all these battles in May, June and July, the Zion men and mules were kept steadily at work, and wherever they went it was gratifying to know that they performed their duties satisfactorily. Sometimes little parties of them would be attached to different battalions, and when their tour of a week or ten days' duty was over they would invariably bring back a letter from the Transport Officer to say how well the men had worked, and how well they had behaved when under fire. I have dozens of such letters, which testify to their good work and how well they got on with their British comrades, with whom they were great favourites; the party commanded by Corporal Nehemiah Yahuda was always in great request, as this bright, cheery young N. C. O. had a happy knack of inspiring his men with his own zeal for work and devotion to duty, regardless of all danger.

Sometimes while away from Headquarters on these detached duties a man would get killed. His comrades always brought the body back to camp, and then the whole Corps attended the funeral, which was a very solemn ceremony. Over the grave of each hero whom we buried in Gallipoli was erected a little memorial, the Shield of David, with his name and the date of his death engraved underneath. Nothing brought the old days of the Bible back more vividly to my mind than to see, when one of my Zion men was wounded, how his friends would literally fall on his neck, weep, and embrace him most tenderly. The outward expression of such emotion as I have witnessed is of course impossible for us Westerners, but I doubt if our feelings are not harrowed all the more by the rigid restraint which we perforce place on them.

The gallant Captain Trumpledor differed from his compatriots in this respect, and I never once saw him give way to any of these emotions. On the contrary, he would remark to me over the body of a badly wounded Zionist: "Ken, ken! (Hebrew for "Yes, yes!") *A la guerre comme à la guerre!*" And I must say that he himself bore a bullet wound through his shoulder with the greatest fortitude, carrying out his duties as if nothing had happened and absolutely refusing to go into hospital. I am glad to say he made a speedy and good recovery.

A couple of my Zionists were not quite so brave as the Captain, for I observed them one day, when we were being somewhat heavily shelled, making tracks for the beach for all they were worth.

Their flight reminded me of a story which I had heard, of an Irish soldier at the Battle of the Boyne, who, relating to a friend how his Captain, before leading them to the charge, said: "Now, boys, strike for your King, your country, and your home." "Some of the fools," said the Irishman, "struck for their King and country, but I struck for home!"

I am glad to say that the valour shown by some of my men made up for the lack of it shown by others. No one could be a braver or a better soldier than Nissel Rosenberg, who, through shot and shell, led his mules with their loads of ammunition right into the firing line, when all others, both Jewish and British—for both were there—made a strategic and hurried movement to the rear. I was watching this myself, and, as I considered it very plucky of him to go forward with his much-needed loads of ammunition, while men were being killed all round him, I recommended him for the D. C. M., a distinction he well deserves. He escaped all wounds that day, but a fortnight later, when again on his way to the trenches, he was severely wounded by a piece of shell; I am glad to say he made a good recovery and is still going strong. In appreciation of his gallant services, I promoted him to the rank of sergeant.

It must not be supposed that we only came under fire on specific occasions. It broke upon us at all times, night and day, without warning. In these "strafes," as we used to call them, many men and mules were killed and wounded.

During one such "strafe," I can even now see Gye and myself running across a couple of hundred yards of fire-swept ground to the rescue of two stricken men, and I should not like to say the number of times we both had to throw ourselves down and grovel on the ground, while shells plunged round us, making holes big enough for our graves and covering us with dirt and gravel. We luckily got through without a scratch and helped to get the wounded men removed, as fast as ever we could, out of danger.

Both were very badly injured, and I never expected to see either of them alive again; one, indeed, Corporal Frank Abraham, died soon after we got him to the hospital; the other, who seemed even more severely wounded, with two bullets through his back, and his thigh smashed to pulp, I was surprised to find in a fair way to recovery, when I visited my sick and wounded men in hospital during a recruiting trip to Alexandria. The poor fellow, when he saw me, seized my hand and embarrassed me by covering it with kisses, saying that but for my lifting him out of that dangerous fire-zone he would certainly have been killed. I was surprised to see that the man remembered that I had been there to help him, as he was in such agony at the time that I did not think he would have remembered or known what was going on around him. I reminded him that he owed quite as much gratitude to Lieutenant Gye as to me, for we had both helped to get him away.

I must mention here, however, that, as a rule, Gye would take on much greater risks to rescue a mule than a man, for which on one occasion he was highly commended by General Hunter-Weston.

Many of the Zionists whom I had thought somewhat lacking in courage showed themselves fearless to a degree when under heavy fire, while Captain Trumpledor actually revelled in it, and the hotter it became the more he liked it, and would remark: "Ah, it is now *plus gai*!"

It must not be supposed that all the Zionists were saints, or that I did not have my times of trouble and difficulty with them, because some would occasionally murmur and hanker after the "flesh-pots of Egypt." They were, indeed, true descendants of those forefathers of theirs who wandered in the wilderness, and whom Moses had so often to chide severely for their stiff-neckedness. Now Moses, in his dealings with his troublesome children, had a tremendous pull over me, because, when my men grumbled about lack of water, I could strike no rock and make it gush forth for them, neither when the meat and food were scarce could I call down manna or quails from Heaven, nor was there any black cloud to interpose and hide us from the devastating fire of our enemy. Although Moses had these Divine aids, yet his task in shepherding over half a million of people through a barren wilderness was truly gigantic and could only be compared to mine as the ocean to a bucket of water; with that great example before me I felt it was up to me not to fail in shepherding through our trials the little host confided to my charge, so, like Father O'Flynn with his flock, I kept my children in order by:

"Checkin' the crazy ones,
Coaxin' unaisy ones,
Liftin' the lazy ones on with the stick."

I found that the racial characteristic of the Israelite made it necessary to hold him in with a thread light as silk and yet strong as a steel cable, and it required a tremendous amount of tact and personal influence to weather the various little storms which sometimes threatened to wreck our family life.

There was great excitement amongst the Zionists when I told them that the much coveted reward for bravery, the Distinguished Conduct Medal, had arrived from England for Corporal Groushkousky, and had been forwarded to me by the Commander-in-Chief. The Corps was paraded in the afternoon and marched to the Headquarters Camp, where General Stopford, the General Officer in Temporary Command of the 8th Army Corps, inspected the men, shook hands with all the officers and finally had Corporal Groushkousky out to the front, and, after congratulating him warmly on his gallant action, pinned the medal on his breast.

CHAPTER XXII. THE AUSTRALIANS AND NEW ZEALANDERS

Towards the end of July, owing to the numbers killed, wounded and in hospital, the Corps was reduced to less than half its strength, and as, at that time, we had no depot in Egypt to send us recruits, it was obvious that, in the course of another couple of months, this interesting and useful unit would cease to exist, if the present rate of casualties continued. The reduced strength of the Corps having come to the knowledge of Sir Ian Hamilton, I was ordered to proceed to Imbros and report to General Headquarters there. I had an interview with the Commander-in-Chief, and the result was that I was commissioned to go to Alexandria, and, if possible, recruit two fresh troops of Israelites in Egypt, and there establish a recruiting and base depot for the Corps.

A considerable stir had been created throughout the Jewish world when it became known that there was, for the first time in British history, a Jewish unit fighting side by side with British soldiers; and there is no doubt that the sympathy of Jews for the Allies was considerably fostered by the presence of this unit fighting in their ranks.

In proof of this I received letters from Jews, and, indeed, from Gentiles, too, from all parts of the world, letters which showed a deep interest in, and sympathy for, this Jewish fighting unit.

Perhaps the most prominent Gentile from whom I heard was Colonel Roosevelt. I only wish I could publish his heartening letter, but at least I may mention that he was anxious to know if my men made good soldiers, because a relative of his was in command of a battery of artillery in one of the Southern States, and he had reported to the ex-President that, curiously enough, part of it was entirely composed of Jews, who were among the most efficient soldiers in the whole battery.

During my interview with Sir Ian Hamilton, I brought these facts to his knowledge, but I found that he was already well informed of the interest and sympathy which the Zion Mule Corps had aroused among the neutral Jews of the world, as he himself had received letters from prominent Israelites in America, and, among others, one from the editor of the New York Jewish newspaper, *The Day*, asking if such a unit really existed.

Sir Ian Hamilton's reply, which appeared in *The Day*, is as follows:

General Headquarters,
Mediterranean Expeditionary Force.

It may interest you to know that I have here, fighting under my
orders, a purely Jewish unit. As far as I know, this is the
first time in the Christian era that such a thing has happened.

The men who compose it were cruelly driven out of Jerusalem by

the Turks, and arrived in Egypt, with their families,
absolutely destitute and starving.

A complete transport Corps was there raised from them, for
voluntary service with me against the Turks, whom they
naturally detest.

These troops were officially described as the "Zion Mule
Corps," and the officers and rank and file have shown great
courage in taking water, supplies and ammunition up to the
fighting line under heavy fire. One of the private soldiers has
been specially recommended by me for gallantry and has duly
received from the King the Distinguished Conduct Medal.

It will therefore be seen that, in my endeavours to keep the Corps alive, I had a
powerful ally in Sir Ian Hamilton.

I was the guest of the Headquarters Staff in Imbros for a few days, so that I had
an opportunity of studying its ways at close quarters. There was certainly no slacking
here. Work seemed to go on day and night, and the food and drink were almost
spartan in their simplicity, practically nothing but the rations which were served out to
the troops, officers and men alike.

I have heard some criticism levelled at the General for being camped away from
the Army, on a secluded island, but, in my humble opinion, it was by far the best
position for the Headquarters Staff and the Commander-in-Chief, because, owing to
the unfortunate division of the Mediterranean Expeditionary Force into two parts, he
was more in touch, from Imbros, with Anzac and Helles than he could have been in
any other place.

Of course, had the Army been all together, I think to be with it would be the right
place for the Commander-in-Chief. It may suit the temperament of the Japanese
soldier to have his chief hidden miles away from the battlefield, but I do not think that
this plan fits in with the temperament of the British soldier. He likes to see his
General, and he likes to know that his General sees him, and realises from personal
contact the nature of the task he is asking his men to perform.

While I was at Imbros, I made an expedition across the island over hill and dale
to the opposite shore, and it was curious to see the old-world way in which the
Greeks, who inhabit the island, live in these modern, hustling days. There I saw two
women grinding at the mill, and the oxen treading out the corn, just as they did
thousands of years ago throughout all the lands of the East. I found the people
hospitable and kindly, ready to offer the stranger a cool draught of water from a

gushing spring (and this was really delicious after Gallipoli), or a platter of luscious mulberries, which were then in season.

But what, perhaps, interested me beyond all else was the view which, on my return journey, I obtained from the summit of a hill, of the position of the Turkish guns at the back of Achi Baba. With my glasses I could see them perfectly plainly, and could actually make out the gunners as they served the guns. With a powerful telescope this would have made a most excellent observation station, as all the Turkish movements at the back of Achi Baba could be plainly seen from this Imbros hill.

When I left Headquarters at Imbros I took passage on a trawler which called in at Anzac, where the Australian-New Zealand Army Corps were dug into the ridges.

I had, of course, a good view of the position they held on the precipitous cliffs and hills which rose in successive sierra-like ridges from the very seashore, and I could then adequately realise the tremendous feat they had performed in gaining a footing on these heights against such a brave and well-armed foe as the Turks.

I had met the Australians before in March, when I had paid them a visit in their romantic camping-ground under the shadow of the Pyramids, and it was in the same month that I met, on the verandah of Shepheard's Hotel, in Cairo, the chief medical officer to the Australian Army, Surgeon-General Williams, whom I had met in South Africa and London some fifteen years previously.

Thinking that he would remember me, I sat down beside him and opened the conversation by saying: "Any chance of a billet with you, General?"

He looked rather blankly at me and said: "Not a ghost of a chance unless you are an Australian. Who are you anyhow?"

I then told him who I was, upon which his face lit up with welcome, but he would not believe that I could be the same man, and asked me to remove my headgear so that he might have a good look at me, as he said I had grown ten years younger.

"How do you manage to keep your youth?" he demanded.

"Oh," I replied, "it is easily done. An uneventful life and no worries," at which the General, knowing something of my travels and adventures, winked, ordered a couple of whiskies and sodas, and over these we had a long talk about things past, present and to come.

General Williams took me round the hospitals and kitchens out at Mena Camp, where we inspected the ambulances and other things under his charge, and I was much impressed with the completeness with which Australia had equipped the magnificent fighting force which she had sent to the aid of England.

It was a great pleasure to meet Colonel Ryan, a senior member of the Australian Medical Staff, who had served with the Turks as a surgeon in their last war against Russia and was with them all through the siege of Plevna. I had read his most interesting book describing his experiences in that war, and altogether I was delighted to have had the pleasure of meeting this most genial Irish Australian.

Camp life at Mena, for the thirty odd thousand men in training there, was very dull indeed. There was not much to relieve the monotony once the Pyramids had been climbed and the Australian colours had been planted on the summits, save an extra dose of sandstorm. It was no wonder, therefore, that every now and again the troops would invade Cairo in force and paint the city red; in fact, one night they painted it very red indeed, when they held a corroboree round the blazing ruins of a Cairene Courtesan's Temple, which they had given to the flames, because the Priestess had, in some way or other, maladministered the rites!

The Staff of the Australian and New Zealand Expeditionary Force, commanded by General Birdwood, had their Headquarters at Shepheard's, and there I met again young Onslow, of the Indian Cavalry, the General's A. D. C., and one of the nicest and handsomest boys that ever buckled on a sabre. He was not only beloved of men, but the gods loved him, too, and it was a black day for me when I heard he was killed at Anzac.

I thought of all these things as I approached the little landing-stage on the Anzac shore, where, as we dropped anchor close to the beach, we got vigorously shelled by the Turks, whose guns, most artfully concealed, dominated the landing.

In the course of the eight months' sojourn there, these guns were responsible for the deaths of hundreds of the Australians and New Zealanders, who were killed while they worked at loading and unloading the stores and ammunition, which were constantly poured into Anzac. In spite of this shell-fire, all through the hot weather scores of men might be seen swimming about and thoroughly enjoying themselves in the water. A look-out man was kept and when he reported a shell coming all dived until the explosion was over.

There are many good stories told of the Australians and their want of reverence for the Staff and their love for the General.

On one occasion, while a dignified and very portly British Staff Officer, who had been having a swim, was drying himself, an Australian came by, and, giving him a hearty smack, said: "Hallo, old sport, you look about ready for the knife. Have you been getting into the biscuit-tin?"

Whatever the Australians may have lacked in what soldiers know as discipline and etiquette they more than made up for by their fearlessness and utter contempt of death in the fight. The very fact that they had gained a footing on these precipitous crags in the face of a desperate resistance showed that they were a race of supermen.

In vain did the Turks, time after time, hurl themselves at them in an attempt to drive them into the sea. The Turks would charge, crying: "Allah! Allah!" The Australians would respond by leaping on the parapets of their trenches, shouting: "Come on, you blighters, and bring him with you." They fear nothing—God, Man, Death, or Devil!

When we eventually plant our flag triumphantly on Gallipoli, the flag of Australia and New Zealand must float in the place of honour upon the Anzac peaks, for here, in their shadows, at peace forever, lie thousands of their bravest sons.

After a few hours my trawler weighed anchor and we steamed south for Helles, which we reached in a couple of hours.

The skipper was a north of Ireland man, and he told me much about the arduous life which the men in the trawlers and mine-sweepers led. During the first attack upon the Dardanelles some of these went through a perfect hell of shell-fire, in fact, right through the Narrows. For eight months, scores of them were constantly on the perilous work of mine-sweeping round Helles and the islands, or carrying troops to and fro; and all this time they were daily under fire, or, during the night, with all lights out, risking themselves and their vessels. More than one sweeper, with all its crew and living freight, came to a sad and sudden end through collision in the dark.

As we neared the landing-stage I spied a new kind of warship for the first time, and as we passed close to her I saw her elevate the muzzles of the two great guns with which she was armed and let fly a brace of shells at the enemy's batteries on Asia. This was the coming of the unsinkable Monitor, armed with her terrible fourteen-inch guns. I don't know how accurate her shots were, but the Turkish gunner who replied was a marvel, for, with his third shot, I saw him strike the deck of the Monitor plump amidships. I heard afterwards that this shell went through all the decks and stuck in the keel plate. By a great piece of good luck no damage was done, as it did not explode.

When I reached the camp of my Zion men I held a parade and told them how interested Sir Ian Hamilton was in the Corps, and how he wished it to be kept up, and with that view had ordered me to proceed to Alexandria to recruit two new troops of their co-religionists. I asked them all to be good boys while I was away, and to work as well for Lieutenant Gye, who would command them in my absence, as they had always worked for me, and in this way keep up the reputation of the Zion Corps.

CHAPTER XXIII. VOYAGE TO EGYPT

To assist me in recruiting, I decided to take with me Claude Rolo, Captain Trumpledor, and Corporal Groushkousky, D. C. M. At 2 P. M. on the 25th July we steamed away from Cape Helles in a little trawler and without adventure arrived at Lemnos at about 7 P. M. We immediately went on board the Staff Ship the *Aragon* in order to get a warrant for our passages to Alexandria.

I must say that I was astonished to find such a splendid Royal Mail Line Steamer as the *Aragon* anchored idly in Mudros harbour, merely to provide quarters for the Lines of Communication Staff. She must have been costing thousands of pounds per week and might have been doing much more useful work on the high seas, where there was a shortage of ships of all kinds.

I have no doubt there were many good men aboard who would prefer to have roughed it on the island in tents, as did the members of Sir Ian Hamilton's Headquarters Staff at Imbros, and there was no reason, so far as I know, why they should not have camped on Lemnos.

It was twenty-four hours before we could take ship for Alexandria, so, during the interval, I went to call on a naval officer who held an important Staff appointment, and who happened to be at the moment in Mudros harbour.

I found the same old difficulty of getting about in the harbour from one ship to another, and it was only due to the courtesy of the Captain commanding the *Aragon*, who kindly placed his boat, cox, and crew at my disposal, that I was enabled to visit my friend. It was a lovely moonlight night as we skimmed across the shimmering water and it was not long until I found myself on the quarter deck of the "———."

My naval friend had just finished dinner when I got aboard, and was most sympathetic and helpful when I told him some of the things which were troubling my mind, and which I had specially come to lay before him. I was anxious to get him to use his influence to send more lighters and more tugs to assist in the disembarkation of stores at Helles. The landing officer there, just before my departure, had begged of me to do what I could in this respect with somebody in authority, as he said he had made repeated requisitions for more tugs and lighters, but all in vain. I was anxious, too, because the pier which had been built by the sappers was of a very flimsy nature, and I knew that the first storm that arose would wash the whole thing away, and then, unless there was a good store of provisions, ammunition, forage, etc., on shore, it would be a very bad look-out for those of us on the Peninsula. As a matter of fact the pier was washed away later on, and for some time the horses and mules were on half rations, and we ourselves were threatened with a shortage of food, but, mainly owing to the excellent arrangements made by Brigadier-General Coe, the head of the Supply and Transport Department, Colonel Striedinger, and other members of his efficient Staff, no breakdown ever occurred.

My naval friend was not over pleased when I told him about this shortage of boats and tugs, and led me to understand that the Navy had supplied everything which the Army had demanded.

It is of vital importance, when our Army and Navy work together, as so often happens, that the Staffs of both should pull together. I think this could be ensured if a capable naval officer, having the entire confidence of the Admiral on the spot, were attached to the General's Headquarters, and a capable military officer, in whom the General placed implicit reliance, were put on the Admiral's Staff; these two officers working together for the common good would obviate all friction. Of course, I am aware that naval and military officers are interchanged on the Staff, but juniors are not good enough for this; they should be senior men who could speak with authority, and whose opinions would carry weight.

The position of the island of Lemnos, some forty miles southwest of the Dardanelles, makes it an important strategic point, more especially as it possesses a magnificent harbour which, with very little trouble and expense, could be made practically impregnable. I sincerely hope that we will retain possession of this island for, with it as a naval base, the Dardanelles can be bottled up at any moment, and the whole of the adjacent seas dominated.

Turkey at present still claims the island. It should therefore be annexed by us as some small compensation for the Gallipoli failure.

On the following day at 7 P. M. we got on board a transport bound for Australia, via Port Said. I found myself the Senior Officer on board, and therefore had to take command of the troops, and among my other charges were some fifty nursing sisters, who had been brought to Lemnos direct from England, and were now being transferred for duty to the military hospitals in Egypt.

Soon after I got aboard we weighed anchor, and I then put the ship's adjutant to the task of detailing to their boats every individual on the ship for whom I was responsible, as I knew there were hostile submarines six or seven hours out from Lemnos, and I wished to be as ready as possible in case of an attack.

At nine o'clock I got the Captain to sound the alarm, when everybody rushed and stood by their own particular boat; I then made a minute inspection, looked over the list of names boat by boat, and by ten o'clock all knew their proper places.

The night was hot, so laying a blanket on the deck, I slept on it there. I was awakened out of a deep sleep by a loud explosion. I leaped up instantly, not yet quite wide awake, saying to myself, what a funny time for an aeroplane to drop a bomb. The next instant I realised that I was at sea, and it flashed through my mind that we had been torpedoed. As I looked over the side, I saw a shell explode a mile or so away, over and beyond a submarine which, in the bright moonshine, could just be made out. The report which had roused me was a shot which had been fired from our own 4.7-inch gun fixed on the stern of the ship. The vessel was instantly swung round so as to present as small a surface as possible to the submarine, and we made off as fast as the ship could steam. A British war-vessel of some kind came up in a few minutes, and we saw and heard nothing more of the submarine, but during the few minutes while the alarm lasted, things were pretty lively on board our transport, and many of the nurses rushed to the side to see what had happened, but there was no sign of alarm or panic among them; they took it all as a matter of course, and seemed quite disappointed when we reached Port Said without further adventure.

CHAPTER XXIV. RECRUITING IN EGYPT

We were detained one night in Port Said, and the following morning made our way by rail to Alexandria. It was an interesting journey because it took us along the Suez Canal as far as Ismalia, where we saw all the defences and the troops guarding it, and also the precautions taken by the householders along the bank, who had turned their homes into little sand-bagged forts. It was on this journey that I saw, for the first time, the celebrated battlefield of Tel-el-Kebir where General Wolseley crushed Arabi Pasha and his army, and there the graves of British and Egyptian soldiers who fell in the battle may be seen from the railway carriages. This journey to Alexandria is rather a roundabout one, for it is necessary to go almost to Cairo before reaching the Cairo to Alexandria line. However, we eventually reached Alexandria in the afternoon, and Claude Rolo took me to the house of his mother, Mrs. J. Rolo, one of the kindest and best ladies it has ever been my good fortune to meet. Here, in this most comfortable and luxurious house, I was made to feel thoroughly at home. While there, I, unfortunately, had a rather severe attack of fever, but thanks to Mrs. Rolo and her nieces, especially "the angel Gabrielle," I was soon restored to health.

My first duty was to see General Sir John Maxwell at Cairo and get his consent and help in raising new recruits for the Zion Mule Corps.

When I arrived in Cairo, however, in the afternoon, I found that I could not see the General until the next morning, so I determined to go and see a friend in hospital, but in which hospital? That was my difficulty.

As I was standing in the verandah of Shepheard's Hotel, wondering to whom I could apply for information, up the steps from the street tripped a charming young lady in nurse's costume. "The very thing for me," I said to myself, and without more ado I walked up to her and explained my difficulty and asked her if she could help. She was kindness itself, and took a great deal of trouble to put me in touch with my friend, and through taking her advice I succeeded in my quest.

I saw Miss —— again on several occasions in the hotel, but not being of a forward nature, I kept out of her way. General Williams told me that she was an Australian lady devoting herself to nursing the sick and wounded. I have heard since that she has added beauty to the British Peerage.

While I was in Cairo, I visited the Turkish wounded in the Red Crescent Hospital there, where they were well looked after and seemed most comfortable. I met a very interesting young Turkish officer, the son of Djemel Pasha, with whom I had a long conversation. He had been captured by the Indian Lancers when he was reconnoitring for the attack on the Suez Canal. He told me that he was the only survivor of a party of twelve, and that he himself had received fourteen lance wounds. He was an extremely good type of Turkish officer, and during the short time we were together we became great friends, and on leaving him he took my hand in both his and shook it warmly, saying he hoped we would always be good friends no matter what the politicians might do for our respective countries.

When I saw General Maxwell he did everything necessary to ensure my success in this new endeavour to raise recruits; he summoned the leading Israelitish notables of Cairo to meet me in his office, where he put my needs before them, and requested them to do what was possible in the way of getting suitable men from their community. Two members of this committee took an interest in raising recruits for the corps, Moise Cattaui Pasha and Mr. Jack Mosseri, the latter a well-known Zionist and a great Hebrew scholar, thoroughly imbued with all the best ideals of the Hebrew race. He was a tower of strength to me, and organised meetings in various synagogues throughout Cairo. One such meeting which took place in the beautiful temple in the Mousky I shall never forget. We walked through this celebrated and picturesque part of Cairo to the meeting—and what a walk! the colours, the lights, the sights, and the sounds, were all redolent of the very heart of the East; even Rahab might be seen there looking out of a window; but of all the charms of the Mousky, and it has many, commend me to its smells! There you will find the full fragrance of the East in all its pristine power and glory! Threading our way carefully through the narrow alley-ways, dexterously avoiding babies, donkeys, mules and camels, we at last reached the Temple. We found it packed with people, and on the platform stood the Grand Rabbi of Cairo, a most imposing and eastern-looking personage, and other notables of the city.

Cattaui Pasha and others, whom Mr. Mosseri had interested in the movement, made stirring addresses to the Jewish youths among the congregation. The result of Mr. Mosseri's efforts was that, in the course of a few weeks, some one hundred and fifty Jewish recruits had been obtained from Cairo alone, and these I designated the "Cairo Troop" of the Zion Mule Corps.

I am sure that Mr. Jack Mosseri will be glad to know that the great majority of these men whom he took so much trouble to imbue with the old Hebrew fighting spirit of the heroes of the past, proved courageous and useful soldiers, when, after a brief training, they found themselves before the enemy in Gallipoli.

While I was at Alexandria I was unlucky enough to get my hand crushed under a motor, and as it required a great deal of attention, I used to go to the Greek Hospital every day because it was close to the office where I worked. This hospital was full of our sick and wounded, where they were carefully attended and nursed by an efficient staff of Greek doctors and Greek nurses. I used to go round the wards talking to the men, and they were all perfectly happy and contented, expressing gratitude for the care lavished on them by the Greek ladies of Alexandria. Dr. Petredes attended to my wounded hand, and nobody could have been more kind. One of the Greek sisters told me rather a pathetic story about an Australian. He was a young fellow badly wounded in the leg; the wound got worse and worse, and it was seen that he must die. He was told by the clergyman who came to visit him that his case was hopeless, but he was not in the least bit upset about himself, he only grieved at the sorrow it would give his mother. Knowing that a photograph would be a comfort to her, he asked if a photographer could be brought. When the latter had arrived, the brave lad insisted on being propped up in bed, and then requested the photographer not to snap him until he could get a nice smile on his face, "For," he said, "I would like my mother to know that I am dying quite happy." In a few hours the boy had passed away, but there remained a photograph with a bright, cheery smile as some small consolation for the bereaved mother.

CHAPTER XXV. LIFE IN EGYPT

While I was in Egypt a few things struck me with particular force: one was the inefficiency of the Police of Alexandria; another the appalling callousness of the average Egyptian in his treatment of animals.

It was an amusing sight in Alexandria to watch the police trying to regulate the traffic. The drivers would take absolutely no notice of the policeman's raised hand, and would dash recklessly over the crossing, quite regardless of what might be coming down the cross street. After being flouted in this way, the policeman would leave his beat, run after the driver and, on catching him up, engage in a wordy warfare for five minutes. The same performance would be repeated over and over again as each successive Jehu came furiously along at his best pace.

I also had some experience of the lax methods prevailing in the Passport Department—a most important office in war-time, especially in a country like Egypt, which was simply teeming with spies.

A couple of my men who had been sent from Gallipoli to the Base Hospital at Alexandria, owing to wounds or illness, wished to resign from the Corps and go to America, as they had no desire to return to the Dardanelles. I, of course, could not grant their request, so by some means or other (bribery, no doubt) they obtained a false passport, got on board ship and gave instructions to some friends of theirs to inform me, three days after they had left, that they were on their way to America and hoped I did not mind! To make sure that these rascals were not merely hiding in Alexandria, I carefully investigated the matter and found that one, at all events, had really sailed.

I have referred to the cruelty which the average Egyptian shows in his treatment of animals. To give one glaring example: there is a steep incline over the railway bridge near Gibbari, a suburb of Alexandria. Over this bridge, the slopes of which are paved with smooth stones, rolls a great part of the immense traffic which goes to and from the docks. Almost at any hour of the day one may see half-a-dozen wretched horses hauling overladen carts up this slippery slope, being unmercifully beaten by their drivers, and falling sometimes two or three times before they reach the summit. I say, without hesitation, that such a scandal is a blot on Alexandria, a blot on the police officials, who wink at it, and a blot on the British rulers in Egypt who tolerate such a state of affairs. A couple of thousand pounds should be set aside at once to remedy the grievous sufferings which are daily and hourly inflicted there on our unfortunate dumb friends.

I was told that a Society for the Prevention of Cruelty to Animals flourishes in the country. If a member of it ever goes up and down the Gibbari Bridge, he must surely turn a blind eye on the cruel sights which are to be seen there almost at any time, otherwise he must be shamed forever. This recalls to my mind a story which Gye once told me about a leading light of this Society who was on a visit to Egypt. He made a tour of the Provinces, and at each place he visited he was delighted to find that the officials were most zealous supporters of the Society. As a proof of their keenness for the League, they would conduct him to the public pound and show him numbers of maimed camels, horses and donkeys which they assured him was the day's catch. Of course it was all eyewash, as the wily officials had got news of the coming of the great one, and told the police to lock up the wretched animals for just as long as he was in the place and no longer.

While the Arabs show appalling callousness to the sufferings of animals, they often exhibit intense kindness and affection for each other; more especially does the Arab mother show great love for her child. A pretty story has come down to us illustrating this maternal solicitude. An Arab youth married a maiden whom he came to love passionately, but he had great love for his mother too, and of this the wife was intensely jealous, so much so, that she told him one day that she could never love him fully while his mother lived, and that the only way for him to secure her affections was to kill his mother and bring her heart as a peace-offering. The wretched youth, blinded by passion, committed this terrible crime, and, concealing his mother's heart within his gown, he ran swiftly to present it to his wife. On the way he tripped and fell heavily, and, in doing so, the heart fell to the ground. On picking it up to replace it, the heart said to him, "My poor boy, I hope you did not hurt yourself when you fell."

I related this story to a friend in London, and he said: "Now I will tell you a story of filial piety on the part of an English boy. He possessed a dog of which he was passionately fond, named Paddy. One day a cart ran over Paddy in the street, and he was picked up dead. The boy's mother broke the dreadful news to her little son while he was having dinner, saying how sorry she was to have to tell him that poor Paddy was killed. The boy was not very much concerned, and went on eating his pudding. Later on, however, in the nursery his Nana condoled with him on the loss of his pet, whereupon he raised a tremendous outcry, sobbing and weeping bitterly. His mother rushed up to see what was the matter, and on finding he was weeping for the dog, said, 'But, darling, I told you at dinner-time that Paddy was killed, and you didn't seem to mind much.'

"'Oh, mammy,' he sobbed, 'I thought you said Daddy—not Paddy.'"

Thinking this would be a good story to tell a little boy that I know very well, I related it to him, but as he took it very gravely, I asked him whether he saw the joke, and he said, "No." Now he possessed a black kitten, named "Mike," for which he had a great affection, so I thought I could illustrate my story by saying: "Well, now tell me which would you rather see run over and killed—Mike or Daddy?"

Having given long and serious consideration to this problem, and with a troubled look on his little face, he, after a great inward struggle, at last said: "I *think* Mike."

During the time I was in Alexandria an attempt was made there on the life of the Sultan of Egypt, not the first attempt, by any means. Now the Sultan is a kindly, good-natured ruler, having the welfare of Egypt and the Egyptians thoroughly at heart; there is nothing whatever of the tyrant about him, and therefore there is no excuse for attempting his life. I happen to know that the Sultan was not at all anxious to accept the dignity which was thrust upon him, but since he has fallen in with the policy of England, it is the duty of England to protect him and uphold him by every means in her power. Let it be known that in case of any further attempt stern measures will be taken, not only on the perpetrator of the crime, or the attempted crime, but on the family and relatives of the criminal, and also on the leading members of any political society to which he belonged—because, of course, they are all in league with each other and know perfectly well what is going on—and if they knew that they would be punished as well as the criminal they would take good care either to dissuade him from the crime or give timely warning to the authorities. If they fail to do this, their property should be confiscated to the State, and if the crime were perpetrated from a hired house, then the owner of the house, who had let it, should be severely punished, because in Egypt the only policy that is understood by the criminal agitator is two eyes for one eye, and a whole row of teeth for one tooth; and the sooner our pusillanimous politicians realise this the better it will be for Egypt, the Egyptians, and the continuance of our rule there. As ex-President Roosevelt said in his vigorous and memorable speech at the Guildhall, we should either "govern Egypt or get out." It is impossible to govern such a country on the milk-and-water policy so loved by invertebrate politicians.

I was privileged, while at Alexandria, to meet on many occasions Prince Fuad, the brother of the Sultan, and it was at one of his many interesting and hospitable receptions, for which he is famous, that I had the opportunity of being presented to His Highness the Sultan. When, however, I looked through the windows of the room where the Sultan was receiving, I saw that he did not appear to be very well (it was soon after the attempt had been made on his life), and there was such a throng waiting to be presented that I determined that I, at least, would save him the fatigue of a handshake. There were compensations for my solicitude for the Sultan, because at that very moment I was talking to a most charming and interesting lady, whose people had hailed from the famous city of the Caliphs, Baghdad, and although her ancestors came from that dusky neighbourhood, she herself was fair as a lily, had gloriously red hair, and was withal as entertaining as Scheherazade. At this same entertainment I saw standing before my eyes and talking to the Sultan a lady whom I took to be Cleopatra herself returned to life. I was amazed to see some one really alive so like the picture of the famous Queen of Egypt, and yet there she was within a few feet of me, carrying on an animated conversation with the Sultan. I came to know "Cleopatra" and her husband very well indeed during my stay in Egypt, and I spent many an enjoyable evening under their hospitable roof. And what a delightful couple they were! I shall never forget a little impromptu concert which took place one night as we sat out under the rustling palms in the soft moonlight. Cleopatra's husband melted all our hearts by singing, in his low, sweet voice, "Un peu d'amour." It prompted me to make the ungallant remark to Cleopatra that I really did not know which of them I liked the better, and ever afterwards she whimsically pretended to be hurt at the lack of discernment which I had shown.

Now, Cleopatra, before I bid you good-bye, I will only say that I am glad you did not live in the days of the Pharaohs, because if you had, I am sure you would have been given to the crocodiles, for you must know that once a year, in those barbarous, far-off times, there was chosen for that sacrifice the most lovely and the most perfect maiden in all Egypt.

It was at some reception or other in Egypt that I met, about this time, an officer who had been on the Staff of the 29th Division in Gallipoli. Riding about the Peninsula as we both did, we met practically every day during two or three months, and although we rode together and were quite good friends, I never knew what his name was, and I never tried to find out, as I am not of an inquisitive nature. However, one day he disappeared and his place in Gallipoli knew him no more. I thought it was very likely he had been killed, because his duties often took him into perilous places— indeed, any and every place in Gallipoli was perilous in those days. At all events, here I met him safe and sound, on which I heartily congratulated him. A little later he asked to be introduced to a friend of mine who was also at the reception, so I was compelled to confess that I had not the foggiest notion as to his name. "My name is B——," he replied; and on asking him if he was any relation of ——, mentioning a well-known public man in England, with whom a few days before I left home I had been walking up and down Rotten Row, "Oh, yes," said he; "that's my father!"

My Gallipoli friend was, unfortunately, on the Persia when she was sunk without warning in the Mediterranean, and went down with the ship; but his time was not yet, for he luckily came up again, and was numbered with the saved, for which Allah be praised.

I hope the reader will not run away with the idea that I spent my time in Egypt in a round of festivities and riotous living. It was, as a matter of fact, very much the reverse, because even when I went to these receptions I combined business with pleasure by getting the people I met there to help me to get recruits and to interest themselves in the Zion Mule Corps.

CHAPTER XXVI. RETURN TO GALLIPOLI

I was very impatient to get back to Gallipoli and made several applications to the Staff both by letter and by telegram to do so, but it takes a long time for the machine to move! At last I received the anxiously looked for orders for myself and my new men to embark.

I had a little trouble with a member of the Staff before I left, and, as it illustrates the pettiness of some men even when great events are at stake, I think it is worth recounting. I had sent him my embarkation return, showing the number of officers and other ranks bound for the Dardanelles. In the meantime a telegram arrived from Gallipoli asking for two of my officers to be sent there immediately. I had them on board and on their way to the front within four hours of the time I read the message. Two days afterwards when I came to embark, I had with me my men and one other officer, but the red-tape, red-tabbed acting Staff man objected to this officer going, as he said my original application was for three officers only, and of these, he said, "Two have already gone; you make the third, therefore the other officer cannot go; he must be left behind to look after the men at Wardian Camp." It was in vain that I pointed out to him that this officer would be of little use at Wardian, but that he was invaluable to me, as he knew the various languages of the men, which I did not, and that I could not very well get on without him. He was obdurate, so I said that, as I must have the officer with me, I would, if necessary, go and see the General and get his sanction. On hearing this threat he took counsel with another red-tab man, whose official designation entitled him to write half the letters of the alphabet after his name, and who, from the little I saw of him, was, I consider, fully entitled to three or four more! These two tin gods, having privily consulted together, issued a *ukase* to the effect that it would be impossible to allow the officer to accompany me to Gallipoli. "All right, then," I said; "there is nothing for it but to see the General, as I must have this officer." This meant that I had to motor some three miles and lose a lot of precious time in order to outwit these ruddy obstructionists, a thing I was determined to do at all costs. When I got to the General's office, I first interviewed his Staff Officer, Major Ainsworth, one of the most sensible and helpful staff officers it has been my luck to come across during the whole campaign. On my proceeding to tell him what I wanted, he said: "Oh, I know all about it. Major —— has already telephoned to me that you were on the way, and has said that, in his opinion, you should not be allowed to embark your extra officer." I remarked to Major Ainsworth that it appeared to me that some of the Staff were only there to obstruct, and I repeated that this man was necessary to me for the efficiency of my Corps, and that it was much more to the point to have efficient officers in Gallipoli, rather than to leave them behind kicking their heels in idleness in Alexandria. This had the desired effect on a sensible man like Major Ainsworth, who tactfully told Major —— that I must have the officer with me that I wanted; and so the incident was closed.

On embarking for Gallipoli for the second time I found that I had 1,100 men on board, made up of 102 different units, many of them without officers, and as I was again the senior on board, I had to take command of the whole, and jolly glad was I to know that I would only be responsible for such a heterogeneous collection for two or three days. The first thing that I discovered on going aboard was that for the 1,100 men we had only boat accommodation for 700 in the event of the ship being sunk. I asked the skipper if he usually put to sea in war-time, when submarines were about, with an inadequate supply of boats, and I refused to sign the clearing papers to say that I was satisfied with all the arrangements on board ship. The captain fully agreed with me; he anchored the vessel in the outer harbour, and we went back together next morning and interviewed the naval authorities, who were furious at the delay in sailing and at my demand for more boats, but at the same time promised to send them out to us in the course of an hour or two, and as soon as they arrived and were stowed away on the deck, we sailed for Lemnos.

I am very thankful that we dodged the submarines on the way, because with such an overcrowded vessel, with so many different units, most of them without officers, and hardly standing room for everybody, and with very inadequate means of getting boats out, I fear that there would not have been many survivors had the vessel been sunk. I issued orders to all on board never to part with their life belts, as they would have to depend on them principally, and not on the boats, for their lives. We were lucky to escape, for just about this time the transport *Ramadan* was sunk with heavy loss of life. It passes my comprehension that ship-owners should be allowed to continue the antiquated methods of boat lowering which are still in existence. How many hundreds of lives have been lost owing to the stupid method in use! Ropes, blocks and tackle are fixed to the bow and stern of each boat, and to ensure that it should reach the sea on an even keel the men using both sets of tackle must lower away at exactly the same rate. What actually happens in any time of excitement is that one rope is lowered much more quickly than the other, with the result that the unfortunate occupants are tilted into the sea and drowned. It would be a simple matter to lower boats by means of one rope only, and this method should be made compulsory on all ship-owners.

Captain Williams of the Munsters was my ship's adjutant. I believe he was the only surviving officer who had landed from the *River Clyde* on that memorable morning of the 25th of April; he had gone through that desperate fight, and had been engaged in every battle on the Peninsula since that date, and yet had come through it all unscathed. He must have borne a charmed life, and I sincerely hope his luck will stick to him to the end. He practically did all the work of the ship for me, and I never had a more efficient adjutant.

We reached Lemnos in safety, and got into the harbour at dusk, just before the entrance was blocked up, because, of course, the harbour mouth was sealed every night from dark to dawn, owing to the fear of submarines. We lay at anchor all night and most part of the next day, and, as nobody seemed to take the slightest notice of our arrival, the captain and I sailed across the harbour in a tiny boat, although the sea was far from calm, and, on reaching the *Aragon*, I reported myself to a gentleman in an eye-glass, whom I had never seen before and never want to see again. He was very "haw haw," and said that I had no business to leave my ship until the military landing officer had been aboard. I remarked that we had been waiting in the harbour so long that I thought perhaps the military landing officer was dead, and so I had come myself to report our arrival. With that I left him and returned to the ship, and soon afterwards we were boarded by the landing officers, and the 1,100 men were drafted off to their different units, I going with mine on a trawler to Cape Helles. We arrived at Lancashire Landing on a beautiful calm moonlight night, and were received with joyous shouts of "Shalom" (the Hebrew form of salutation) from the veterans of the Corps.

I missed the face of Lieutenant Gorodisky from among those who greeted me, for, alas, he had died during my absence from an illness contracted owing to the hardships of the campaign. By his death the Corps suffered a severe loss. He had resigned from an important and lucrative post in Alexandria and enlisted as a private soldier in the Zion Mule Corps. His ability and soldierly qualities soon raised him to officer's rank, and he was one of the best and most useful in the Corps. Like all Israelites he was passionately fond of music, and it was he who wrote out for me the Hatikvoh, the music of which has been arranged for me by Miss Eva Lonsdale and will be found in the Appendix. He told me once that, though the Germans claimed that they were the most musical nation in the world, yet all their best musicians were either Jews or had Jewish blood in them. His death was a sad blow to his widowed mother, as he was her only child. Madame Gorodisky may, however, be proud to have been the mother of such a noble character, and it will, I trust, be some consolation to her to know that he was held in the highest esteem by every officer and man, not only in the Zion Mule Corps but also by those who knew him in the French and British regiments among whom we were camped.

CHAPTER XXVII. BEELZEBUB

I found, on my return in September, that life on the Peninsula was much less strenuous than when I had left for Egypt at the end of July. The Turks must have been very short of ammunition, for few shells were fired for the first five or six weeks after our arrival. I was able to have drills and parades in the open, exposed to the full view of Achi Baba and Krithia—a thing which would have been out of the question in the early days. It was quite a pleasure to be able to ride about all over the Peninsula even to within a few hundred yards of the Turkish trenches without being shelled. Of course, in the days when the Turks had plenty of ammunition, they thought nothing of wasting half a dozen rounds on a solitary horseman, and many a time have I had to gallop at breakneck speed to avoid the shrapnel which they peppered me with on many occasions. I was very glad indeed that shells were rather scarce, as it gave my recruits time to get into shape and get used to the conditions of warfare.

The new Cairo men took to the life very kindly, and soon burrowed themselves well into the ground and adapted themselves to cave dwelling as to the manner born.

In the evenings, when our day's toil was ended, we had concerts round our camp fires and enjoyed ourselves as much as it was possible to do under the circumstances; in fact, at times we used to forget that we were at war.

The camp-fire sing-songs were rather weird affairs—songs in English (Tipperary, for choice), French, Russian, Hebrew and Arabic—the two latter made rather melancholy by the plaintive wail of the East. Some of the men were first-rate Russian dancers and expert wrestlers, so we had many excellent little side-shows.

The concerts were always ended by singing "God Save the King," the Marseillaise (for many French soldiers would be present), the Russian Anthem, and last of all the Maccabæan March.

We had many visitors to our quaint polyglot lines; a strenuous lieutenant all the way from Canada often called on us, and I was indebted to him for an invitation to come and try my hand at tent-pegging on a beautiful tan track which he had made and at which various officers used to meet to run a course.

Now I used to be rather good at the game, and I think I rather surprised my Canadian friend, Maurice, when, in answer to his bantering challenge: "Now, Colonel, show us how it's done!" I took every peg for which I tried. It was good to find that one could still ride straight and depend on eye, hand and arm, and that the spear-point could be made to strike the peg as squarely and as surely as of old.

There was not a great deal of work to be done in these days, as there was now any amount of other Transport which took much of the weight off our shoulders.

The lack of steady hard work made the mules very frisky, and some of them were regular demons. We had one which was rightly named Beelzebub, for he was indeed a prince of devils, and I veritably believe he made all the other mules laugh when he kicked one or other of the N. C. O.'s or men. He had an extraordinary cat-like faculty of being able to plant fore and hind feet into one's ribs practically simultaneously, while at the same moment he would make a grab at one's head, emitting all the while strange noises and terrifying squeals! He pinned me in a corner one day, apparently to the delight of the other mules, and I was glad to get out of it alive! In order to make him pay a little more respect to his commanding officer for the future, I ordered him to be tied up to a tree and kept for a day without food or water. This, however, did not fall in with Beelzebub's theory of things, so he gnawed through the rope in the night and then made for the forage stack, where, to make up for lost time, he ate about six mule rations!—at which the other mules did not laugh!

No one was over-particular about Beelzebub's safety, as he was not what might be called popular, so instead of being put down with the others in a dug-out, where indeed he would have kicked them to bits, he was generally left by himself in about the most exposed position that could be found for him in the camp, and I am quite certain that both Jewish and Gentile prayers went up for his speedy annihilation by a Turkish shell; but Beelzebub bore a charmed life. Shells hopped all round him, cut in two great trees which sheltered him, excavated enormous caverns at his very heels, but the only effect they had on Beelzebub was to rouse his ire and start him off on a fresh kicking bout. At last a chunk of shell hit the ground close to him, bounced up and "ricked" off his ribs, making a wound, not very serious, it is true, but still not exactly calculated to improve his diabolical temper.

I sent him off to the sick lines to have his wound dressed. Now I never could find out what he actually did to the veterinary surgeon who tried to doctor him there, but this officer wrote a polite little note requesting me to be so very kind as to remember in future that his hospital was for sick mules—not for Man-Eaters!

I have already mentioned that on the night of my return to Gallipoli from Egypt a brilliant moon was shining, and by the light of it I saw great mounds of earthworks thrown up just to one side of our lines. On looking closer, I found that these were the emplacements for four heavy French guns of 9.6-inch calibre.

I cannot say that I was over-pleased at the sight, because I knew that the moment they opened fire their position would be seen from Achi Baba, and the shells which the Turks would be bound to hurl at them would be more than likely to miss the battery and hit my men and my mules.

Two French officers were in charge of the siege pieces, Captain Cujol and Lieutenant La Rivière, both exceedingly nice men with whom we made great friends. The gallant captain was a great horseman, and I often delighted him (for he had no horse with him) by mounting him on one of mine, and together riding over the Peninsula. Lieutenant La Rivière, who was a much-travelled man, often entertained us with stories of his wanderings and adventures in Arabia, Abyssinia and the Soudan in the long evenings after we had all dined together in our cosy little dug-out.

While I was away recruiting in Egypt the glamour of the Horse Artillery had fallen upon Gye, and, furthermore, Davidson and other officers of L Battery had beguiled him, so that soon after my return he asked me if I would let him go to the Gunners. I was glad to recommend him for the transfer, for I felt that with his sound common sense and good horsemastership he would be of more use to the general cause as a gunner than as a muleteer.

I had two British officers still left with me, and here, too, was a case of good material being wasted on work which could have been equally well done by less brainy men.

Claude Rolo was an eminent civil engineer, and had constructed some of the most important public buildings in Egypt, and, of course, his proper place would have been with the Sappers. His brother, I. Rolo, with his vast business experience in Egypt, should have been employed as purchasing agent for the Army, where his knowledge of local affairs would undoubtedly have saved us tens of thousands of pounds. His talents were wasted merely keeping the records of the Zion Mule Corps Depot at Alexandria. I recommended both for transfer, but I fear their services are still being wasted.

I wonder when we will wake up to the fact that we have plenty of talent if only those in authority would avail themselves of it and use it in the right way.

CHAPTER XXVIII. A FEAT IN GUNNERY

By this time, after many weeks and months of delving, the efforts of our Engineers and other troops to alter the geographical features of the Peninsula began to have effect. Long lines of communication trenches were dug to and fro everywhere. Indeed, the amount of earthwork that was excavated in digging trenches and dug-outs, both at Helles and Anzac, was simply "colossal." If the same amount of digging, trenching and dug-outing had been concentrated into one effort, it would have been possible to make a canal across the narrowest part of the Peninsula, wide enough and deep enough for the *Queen Elizabeth* and the rest of the British Fleet to sail through, without let or hindrance, to Constantinople!

One good thing the diggers did was to make the communication trenches wide and deep enough to give ample cover to horses and mules. In consequence of this, it was now possible to take ammunition and supplies to the front during daylight, and so most of our night work ceased. Small detachments of men and mules were attached to various battalions for transport work, and all over the Peninsula Zion men could be met cantering along on their mules—for they were good horsemen—and they invariably rode when they had a chance. They looked very comical as they galloped along, uttering exulting yells, their faces grimy, caps crammed home on the back of their heads, jacketless and with torn shirts, perched up on the pack saddles, the chains of which clattered loudly at each stride of the mule. Our soldiers, with their usual happy knack for nicknames, christened them the "Allies Cavalry," while a brilliant wit went even one better and dubbed them "Ally Sloper's Cavalry!"

While the men were out on these detached posts, I, of course, visited them at regular intervals to see that they were keeping up the reputation of the Corps and also to hear any reports or complaints they might have to make. It was rarely that a day went by without something odd or amusing, or both, happening at one or other of these detached posts. For example: I had some men stationed up the Gully Ravine, and just before I visited them the Turks had given them a vigorous bombardment which had set fire to the forage which was stored close by the mules. The last of it was being burned up just as I arrived on the scene and, as my men were still lying low in their dug-out, I shouted for the corporal and angrily demanded why they had not saved the forage. He replied: "Turk he fire shells, plenty shells, hot, hot—too bloody hot," which showed that their sojourn with the British Army, if it was doing nothing else, was at least improving their knowledge of classical English!

Although Gye had by this time joined L Battery for duty, he still lived with me in our little dug-out under the great olive tree, which, by the way, now supplied us with excellent olives. Being with the gunners, he would occasionally get early news of an artillery "strafe," which, as a rule, we went together to watch from some commanding position.

I was not surprised, therefore, when one afternoon he came in from the battery and told me there was to be a most interesting "shoot" on in the afternoon, nothing less than the "strafing" of a troublesome Turkish redoubt by the huge guns of one of the Monitors. As this promised to be a rare good show, we sallied forth on our horses, taking the road by X Beach and the Gully Ravine. On reaching our observation post and seeing no sign of a Monitor in the vicinity, I remarked to Gye: "It certainly is a very fine afternoon for a ride, but I don't see much appearance of that 'strafe' you promised to show me."

"I think it will be all right," replied Gye, "there is the Monitor away out at sea," pointing to a speck close over to the Imbros shore, some seven or eight miles away—a mere cockleshell in the distance.

On looking from the speck to the redoubt I said: "It is not a 'strafe' you have brought me out to see but a miracle," because it looked to me that it would be little short of a miracle to hit that small redoubt which, of course, could only be faintly seen from the tops of the Monitor by telescope.

However, I hadn't to wait long for the wonderful sight. Punctually to the moment when it was expected, we saw the Monitor enveloped in great billows of waving clouds of flame and smoke—one of her great 14-inch guns had been fired. Anxiously we watched the redoubt and, incredible as it may seem, the shell only failed to strike it by thirty yards, for at that distance from it a great upheaval of earth could be seen. Again we watched, the Monitor. "Pouf!" went her second gun, this time sending the shell plump into the redoubt. The result was extraordinary. Up went Turks, rocks, timbers, guns, all mixed up in a cloud of smoke, flame and earth—a marvellous shot! Three more followed in quick succession, each one plumping right into the redoubt, pulverising it absolutely out of existence. It was as if a steam-roller had gone over the earthworks. A few more shells were dropped into the fort, just to make sure, and one of these, having struck some hard substance, "ricked" across the Peninsula, over the Dardanelles, and exploded in Asia!

I took off my hat to the man behind the gun on that Monitor. If he is a type of all other gunners in the British Navy, the Germans may as well scrap their fleet without further ado.

After watching this wonderful feat of gunnery, we were riding back towards camp, when we saw running towards us an old soldier of a Scottish regiment in a state of great excitement, apparently having something of importance to impart. I pulled up my horse and asked him what was the matter. He told me in the broadest Scotch that there was a German spy a little further down among the gorse taking notes and sketching the position of a heavy battery which was in position close by the sea. I asked the Scotty how he knew the man was a spy, and he said: "He's goin' on verra suspeecious."

I got him to point out the exact position of the supposed spy and then I arranged with Gye that I would go up and open conversation casually with him, and that if I made a certain signal, he was to gallop off for an escort. I found the "spy" dressed in khaki in the uniform of a Scottish regiment. I opened the conversation by asking if he had seen the magnificent shooting of the Monitor, and carried it on until I found out who he was and from whence he had come. I knew that his regiment was forward in the trenches, so I asked him why he was not at the front, and he told me that he was going through a course at the bombing school and so, for the moment, was away from his battalion. He seemed all right, but to make sure I sent Gye over to see the Instructor at the bombing school, which was close by, to find out if such an officer was really there taking a course.

While Gye was away I strolled to the edge of the cliff with the supposed spy who, I was now pretty sure, was what he represented himself to be—a British officer. Down below us on the shore was the body of a dead horse, half in and half out of the sea, and tearing at it was a good-sized shark which we could see very plainly, for the water was beautifully clear. My spy got very keen on seeing this and, borrowing a rifle from a soldier standing near, he made such good shooting at the shark that it speedily gave up its horse-feast and plunged off to the depths in terrified haste. In the midst of the fusillade, Gye came back to say all was well, so bidding my "spy" good-afternoon, we rode off to our camp.

There is no doubt, however, that the Peninsula was alive with spies, and at night, on returning from the trenches, when all the camps would be in slumber, I have repeatedly seen flashes sent up from the British lines towards Krithia, where they would be answered, but although I tried on several occasions to locate the signaller, I never succeeded in doing so. Of course I reported the matter to Headquarters, but whether they were more successful than myself I never learned.

On one occasion, a night or two before we made a big attack, I distinctly saw signals flashed from the neighbourhood of the cliffs by the Gully Ravine, where there was the Headquarters of a Division, to the lines of the Royal Naval Division, from which a signaller answered back; both then signalled to somebody on the hill where the Headquarters Staff of our Army Corps were established, and this signaller in his turn flashed messages up to Krithia, where there was a steady red light shown for a considerable time while the signalling was in progress. I tried to locate the signaller on the Headquarters hill, but failed. I then reported the matter to the Chief Signalling Officer, who told me that whatever lights I had seen were not made by our people, as none of the signallers were out on duty that night. Gye and I found the spot from which the daring spy on the Headquarters hill had been signalling. It was most craftily selected, as it was completely sheltered for three-quarters of the way round, and his light could only be seen from the direction of Krithia; I had not been able to observe it until I came into a direct line between Krithia and the hill.

The tricks and daring of the spy are wonderful! It was common gossip in the Peninsula that a Greek contractor who was allowed to sell some tinned foods, etc., to the soldiers, had in some of the larger tins, not eatables, but carrier pigeons, which he would send off to the Turks on suitable occasions, but whether this is true or not I cannot say for certain. It was rumoured that he was found out and shot.

Some of our fellows used to do the most extraordinary things. A sergeant, thoroughly bored with life in the trenches, thought he would like to break the monotony by having a look at the Turks, so, shouldering his rifle, he sauntered over to the enemy trenches and looked in, and there saw five Turks, three sitting together smoking and two others lying down having a rest. He shot all five and then doubled back to his own trench, escaping in some marvellous way the hail of bullets that came after him.

Then there was Lieutenant O'Hara of the Dublins, who was always doing some daring feat and showing his contempt of death and the Turks on every conceivable occasion. He won the D. S. O. before going to Suvla, where, alas! his luck deserted him, and he was mortally wounded. O'Hara firmly believed that no Turk could ever kill him, for he thought nothing of sitting up on the parapet coolly smoking a cigarette, while bullets rained all round him. When he had finished his survey of the Turkish line he would get down, but not before.

Another brave man of the Dublins was Sergeant Cooke. If ever there was a dangerous job he always volunteered for it, and was constantly out reconnoitring the enemy's position and bringing in useful information to his officers. He, too, was very lucky for a long time; he was one of the few who escaped all hurt in the original landing, but at Suvla, Sergeant Cooke, while doing a brave deed, was mortally wounded, and, although he must have been in great agony for a couple of hours before he died, he never uttered a groan. Just before the last, he said: "Am I dying like a British soldier?" No soldier ever died more gamely.

CHAPTER XXIX. THE FINDING OF THE SHIELD OF DAVID

Soon after the Bulgarians had thrown in their lot against us, the Turks, who up to this time had been husbanding their ammunition, felt, I presume, that there was now no need to be so sparing in their use of shells, and they therefore took on a much more aggressive attitude.

Turkish bombardments and trench "strafes" once more became the order of the day. Not to let the enemy have everything his own way, we ourselves arranged, late in October, to make a tremendous onslaught on the Turks. One of their trenches, known as H. 12, occupied a somewhat commanding position and had been giving us a lot of trouble. It was decided, therefore, to batter it out of existence.

Sharp to time, at three o'clock on a very "nippy" afternoon, a most terrific cannonade was opened on the doomed trench. Naval guns, French guns, British howitzers and field-pieces rained a devastating fire of high explosives and, as if this were not enough, three huge volcanoes spurted out at three points of the trench, denoting that some great mines had been exploded. While the fire lasted, it was terrific, and the dust and smoke speedily hid all the Turkish trenches, as well as Krithia and Achi Baba, from our view. The infantry were then launched and the trench captured with very little loss.

Trench warfare, dull as it is, for those who prefer a fight in the open, with a good horse under them, is yet not without its moments of fascination, and I often found myself in the thick of a trench "strafe" when I really had no business whatever to be in the neighbourhood.

Gye, Rolo and I were returning from one of these trench fights in mid-October, when we ourselves nearly got "strafed" at Clapham Junction, a well-known spot behind the firing line on our right centre. Our mortars, borrowed from the French, had thoroughly annoyed the Turks and they retaliated by bombarding our trenches with shell-fire. We were pretty safe so long as we remained under cover, but on the way back to camp we caught it rather badly and only saved ourselves by our speedy flight over an exposed piece of ground which we had to cross, where the shells were falling pretty thickly.

One of the most annoying things the Turks did was to mount a big naval gun "somewhere in Asia" not far from Troy—as distances go in Asia. This fiendish weapon had such a high velocity that the shell arrived on us before the report of the gun was heard. The sensation of hearing the shell screaming a few feet over one's head was most unpleasant, and we all looked for the moment that the big French guns in our lines would begin to shoot, as things were very disagreeable for us while "Helen" was in action. This gun was altogether so troublesome that we had christened it "Helen of Troy."

Fortunately, only about one in four of its shells burst, otherwise we should have suffered very heavily, because many of them fell in and around our lines. My men would calmly pick up these unexploded shells and struggle off with them on their shoulders to adorn the entrance of their dug-outs! This used to horrify the French gunners, who were close by and knew the danger of touching such dangerous toys. I am afraid my Zionists thought me somewhat of a tyrant for abolishing these æsthetic aids to the beautification of their subterranean homes!

Now and again, just as a reminder of the rigours to come, we were deluged by a downpour of rain, and then life in the trenches was almost unbearable, for, owing to the subsoil being clay, all the water ran on the surface and speedily filled up every trench, dug-out and hollow; and this discomfort, coupled with mud, filth, too little food and sleep, and too much shells and bombs, made life in Gallipoli more fit for a dog than a man.

As the cold weather was coming on, I determined to build a good stone house for my men, where there would always be a big fire going to keep them warm and to dry their clothes when they came back wet from the trenches. As it was not in our zone, I had to get the permission of the Chief Engineer of the French Army to take some stones from Sedd-el-Bahr village, because it was only there that building material could be obtained. While we were pulling down a house and excavating the foundation, we dug up a slab of marble with a beautiful filigree design carved round the outer edge of it, and in the centre, strange to say, was the Shield of David! The stone must have been very, very old, and how it got there is a mystery. Perhaps it may have been taken from Solomon's Temple in Jerusalem.

My Zion men were delighted at the find and brought the stone in triumph to our camp, and it was kept in the new house as a talisman to ward off the shells. Strange to say, although they fell all round, the building was never touched nor was any one injured in its vicinity.

Our own dug-out was also greatly improved when the weather became bitterly cold. We made the fireplace and chimney-stack out of old kerosene tins, which made a kind of brasier on which we burned charcoal obtained from the refuse heap at the Field Bakery. Altogether, our dug-out was considered to be the cosiest one in the whole Peninsula, as indeed it had every right to be, for was not Claude Rolo, who was our architect and engineer, one of the cleverest civil engineers that ever passed through the Polytechnic in Paris?

Our charcoal fire was very useful in many ways; it made very good toast, for the bread, which up to now had been excellent, began to be sodden owing to the bakery being in the open and, of course, getting the full benefit of all the rain that often came down in torrents; and in addition to the rain the unfortunate bakers were at all times under shell-fire. Although the bread was not up to the usual standard after the rains set in, yet in the whole history of war I do not believe that men and animals have ever been better fed than were the troops, horses and mules during the whole time we were on the Peninsula. The variety of food might perhaps have been bettered, but the quality and quantity on the whole were excellent and reflected the greatest credit on the organisation of the Army Service Corps; in fact, it was the only department where one could say all the time—it had done well. The Ordnance failed at times—failed lamentably in the supply of high explosives for the guns, but this was through no fault of the ordnance officer on the spot, who, I know, took every precaution to ask for every conceivable article months before it was required. Of course, he did sometimes get the needed articles, and sometimes, when it was on its way, submarines would sink the ship, or the ordnance people said the ship was sunk, which amounted to the same thing and covered a multitude of sins. Those submarines saved many reputations! All the sapper supplies, however, might just as well have been sunk, as it was impossible to get the smallest scrap of material, no matter how urgently required, without the most minute details as to what it was for and all about it. There was any amount of stuff one wanted in the Field Park, but when application was made for it the invariable reply was, "It is earmarked for other purposes."

This policy is all very well in normal times, but does not do for war. Some men cannot shake off the petty trammels by which they are fettered in times of peace.

I have no doubt the Turks much enjoyed the use of a considerable amount of this "earmarked" material, which, if it had been issued to us, would have greatly enhanced the comfort of man and beast.

I remember on one occasion being in want of a gallon of tar. Now there was any amount of it in the stores, in fact, one could see it oozing out of the barrels in all directions. I wanted this tar to put on some ropes and sacks filled with sand which I was burying in the ground to make my horse lines and to waterproof some canvas; so I sent a man to the R. E. Park, with a requisition, hoping to get it back in the course of half an hour or so; but no: all he brought back was a letter to say: "Please explain for what purpose you require this gallon of tar." I was so annoyed that I replied: "To make a bonfire when you get the order of the boot." But I have some doubt as to whether this message ever reached its destination, as I had a very diplomatic adjutant.

The officers and men of the corps of Royal Engineers who wore no red-tabs were simply splendid, and it was with admiration that I often watched them at all hours of the day and night, digging trenches, making saps, or putting up barbed wire, right in the very teeth of the enemy—"Second to None."

It is sometimes of vital importance in war to do the exact contrary to all peace tradition; but men get into a groove, get narrow, and often fail to rise to the occasion. I have a good instance of this in mind. A certain officer refused to issue sandbags from his store when they were urgently needed. (This did not happen at Helles.) "They cost sixpence each," he remarked, "and I have got to be careful of them,"—a wise precaution in peace-time, but utterly unsound in war, because a few sandbags at sixpence each might save the lives of several soldiers worth hundreds of pounds, putting it on merely a cash basis.

CHAPTER XXX. BACK TO ENGLAND

Shortly before I left Gallipoli our Staff arranged what the American soldier would call a great "stunt." Materials for a huge bonfire were secretly collected and placed in a commanding position after dark on the heights near the Ægean coast; near to it a mine was laid. At about ten o'clock at night this was purposely exploded, making a terrific report; next moment, according to prearranged plan, the bonfire, which had been liberally saturated with oil and tar, burst into a great sheet of flame which lit up half our end of the Peninsula. Our Staff fully expected that the explosion followed by the great fire would bring every Turk out of the depths of his trench to the parapet in order to see what had happened; so at this moment every gun on the Peninsula, which of course had the range of these Turkish trenches to a yard, loosed off a mighty salvo. Next morning at daylight the Staff eagerly scanned the enemy's parapets, expecting to see them littered with dead—but instead they were somewhat chagrined to observe our old friend the Turkish wag slowly raise a great placard announcing: "No Casualties!"

The Turks were now much more lively in their cannonading, and began once more their hateful tactics of loosing off shells at mounted men.

About a fortnight before I left the Peninsula, I was riding up from Gully Ravine, and, having got to the top of what is called Artillery Road, I met a gun team, and one of the drivers told me to be careful going along the next couple of hundred yards, as the Turks were shelling the short strip of road just ahead. I was walking my horse at the time, and continued to do so, as I felt I was just as safe walking as galloping. In a few moments I heard the report of a gun from behind Krithia, then I heard the scream of a shell coming nearer and nearer, and as I bent my head down to the horse's mane I said to myself: "This is going to be a near thing." The shell whizzed close above my head and exploded a yard or two beyond me, plastering some twenty or thirty yards of ground with shrapnel. My horse took no notice of the explosion, and continued walking on as if nothing had happened. Although I was anxiously on the look-out for another salute from the enemy, I thought, if I just walked on, I would bluff the Turkish observing officer into thinking that, as I took the matter so unconcernedly, he must have the wrong range and it would be useless to go on shooting. It was either that or else he was a sportsman and thought that, as I had taken my escape so calmly, he would not shoot again, for at any rate not another round was fired.

Although I did not know it at the time, Gye had been watching the whole of this episode from a little distance. He had seen the gun team being shelled as it galloped for shelter down to the Gully, and when he saw me emerge he felt pretty sure that I would be fired on as soon as I was spotted by the Turkish gunners. He told me it was most exciting to watch me as I came to the dangerous bit of road, hear the report of the Turkish gun, hear the shriek of the shell as it came along, and then see it go bang, apparently on my head!

As was to be expected, where cannonading and battles were the order of the day, there was little to be seen on the Peninsula in the way of animal or bird life. The cranes which Homer sings of somewhere or other, flew in great flocks down to Egypt, flying almost in the arrow formation of geese when in flight, but with the arrow not quite so regular. I have put up some partridges out of the gorse, between the Gully Ravine and the Ægean, within a hundred yards of where the guns were blazing away for all they were worth. There were a few other small birds about, but very few, if any, warblers. I came across one dead hare, shot by a stray bullet, and I had a glimpse of one live one as it scuttled away in the gorse. The only other four-footed wild thing that I saw in the Peninsula was what appeared to be a cross between the merecat and the mongoose, but slightly larger than the mongoose. It was of a dark reddish-brown colour, thickly dotted over with grey spots. I saw one or two small snakes, but whether they were venomous or not I cannot say, for they glided off into their holes before I could secure a specimen.

A night or two before I left Gallipoli we had a sudden downpour of rain which made the trenches raging torrents, and turned the dug-outs into diving baths; but still our men remained cheery throughout it all; nothing can depress them. The men of L Battery, R. H. A., like all others, were flooded out in the twinkling of an eye, and I watched them, standing in their shirts on the edge of their dug-outs, endeavoring with a hooked stick to fish up their equipment and the remainder of their attire from a murky flood of water four feet deep—all the time singing gaily: "It's a long way to Tipperary."

My escape on Artillery Road was the last serious little bit of adventure I had on the Peninsula, for towards the end of November I got ill, and Captain Blandy, R. A. M. C., packed me off to hospital. My faithful orderly, Corporal Yorish, came with me to the hospital and saw that I was comfortably fixed up for the night. I cannot speak too highly of this man's behaviour during the whole time he was with me in Egypt and Gallipoli. In Palestine he was a dental student, but he could turn his hand to anything, and was never happy unless he was at work.

I spent that night in the clearing station close to Lancashire Landing, on a bed having a big side tilt, with a dozen other officers all round, some sick, some wounded. We had a dim light from a hurricane lamp suspended to a rope, which was tied to the tent poles, and we got a little warmth and a lot of smell from an oil stove, for the weather was now very cold.

At about 4 A. M. I dozed off, and the next thing I remember was a Turk leaning over me, trying, as I thought, to prod me in the face with a bayonet. I made a vicious kick at him which woke me up, and then I discovered that my Turk was no Turk at all but merely the hospital orderly, who was attempting to jab a thermometer into my mouth in an effort to take my temperature. It was 5 A. M. and the hospital machine had begun to work, and whether you are well, or whether you are ill, or whether you are asleep, or whether you are awake, temperatures and medicines must be taken according to rule and regulation.

This same clearing station had seen some very lively times, because it is close to the ordnance stores, and in a line from Asia to W Beach, so that shells used to fall into it both from Achi Baba and from across the Dardanelles. Orderlies and patients had been killed there, and many others had had marvellous escapes. Scores and scores of times have I witnessed the departure of the sick and wounded, which generally took place in the evening, and the clock-like precision with which everything worked reflected the greatest credit on Colonel Humphreys, R. A. M. C., who was in charge of it from the beginning to the end, and on the members of the R. A. M. C. Corps who assisted him. From what I saw of the R. A. M. C. men in Gallipoli, this Corps has every reason to be proud of itself. Of course, at the first landing there was a lamentable medical break-down, and there is no doubt that hundreds of lives were lost because there were not enough doctors, attendants, and stores to go round. Hundreds and hundreds of badly wounded men had to be stuffed anywhere on board transports and sent down to the hospitals at Alexandria with practically no one to look after them, excepting their lesser wounded comrades; but this was an administrative blunder, which does not reflect on the pluck, energy and skill shown by all those R. A. M. C. officers and men with whom I came in contact in Gallipoli.

Colonel Humphreys saw me off on the morning of the 29th of November, and I went down in an ambulance full of officers and soldiers to the French pier at V Beach, the same at which I had landed in April, because our own pier at W Beach had been washed away and could not be used. While we were getting on board the trawler which was to take us to the hospital ship, the Turks put a few shells close round us in their efforts to damage the French works on V Beach. This was their last salute so far as I was concerned, for I never heard another shot fired. They were very good about our hospital ships, and never attempted to do any shooting which would endanger them in any way.

As we rounded the stern of the hospital ship in order to get to the lee-side, as the weather was a bit boisterous, I was interested to see that the ship was called the *Assaye*.

Now during the South African War, I had gone out in this same ship in command of about twelve hundred troops, and it was somewhat odd that I should now see her as a hospital ship and be going aboard her as a patient. I found things very comfortable on board, and certainly it was an immense change to us to find ourselves once more between sheets on a spring bed swung on pivots, so that the patients should not feel the motion of the ship. We were very democratic in the hospital, as generals, colonels, majors, captains, lieutenants and senior N. C. O.'s, some thirty or forty of us in all, were jumbled up together in the ward.

There was only one nursing sister for our ward, an Australian lady, Sister Dixon, who certainly worked like a slave from somewhere about seven in the morning until ten at night. Her task was too severe, and enough to break down any ordinary mortal. She was assisted in the ward duties by Corporal O'Brien, who did what he could to make us comfortable. The night orderly was a big kindly Scotch Highlander, named Mackinnon, almost as tender and sympathetic as a woman, who apologised profusely when he had to wake us every morning at 8 A. M. to take our temperatures and count the beats of our pulse.

The *Assaye* lay off Cape Helles in a blinding blizzard of hail and snow, during which many of the poor fellows in the trenches were, I am told, frozen to death, or, as a lesser evil, got their feet frozen during that very cold spell.

On the 27th we set sail for Mudros, which we reached in about four hours, where we lay at anchor for a day, and there was much speculation as to whether we would be transhipped, or go ashore and be put in hospital on this island, each and all wondering what was going to happen. One or two light cases were put ashore, and then the ship weighed anchor bound for Alexandria, which we reached without adventure on the 1st of December. All of us who were unable to walk were carried ashore by some stalwart Australians, and then we were sandwiched into a motor ambulance, still remaining on our stretchers, and driven off to Ras-el-Tin Hospital, which occupied an excellent position by the edge of the sea. Here I spent fifteen days getting every care and attention from Miss Bond (the matron), and nursing sisters Blythe and Jordon, who looked after the patients in my ward. Ras-el-Tin Hospital is used for officers only, but I noticed that some of the medical officers were somewhat young and inexperienced. This I consider wrong, because in these days the lives of officers are of great importance, and only the best and most experienced medical officers should be employed to look after them, and get them fit for their duties as soon as possible.

My own little experience in this respect may not be out of place here as an apt illustration of what I have just written.

The senior medical officer in charge, a very young temporary captain, without coming to see me, decreed that I was fit and well enough to leave the hospital for a convalescent home. Now, I was just about able to crawl and no more, and the matron and sister who knew the state I was in, told him that I was utterly unfit to leave the hospital. However, without coming to see me, he still remained obstinate, and ordered my kit away, but meanwhile, Colonel Beach, the A. D. M. S. Alexandria, having come to see me, his experienced eye showed him that it would be some months before I should be fit for military duty again, and he told me I should have to go before a medical board, who would dispose of my case. The following day the medical board decided to send me to England, and I was put on board the hospital ship *Gurkha*, which I found very comfortable, with excellent food and a most excellent medical staff, a colonel, three majors, and a captain, all of the Indian Medical Service; and I thought what a pity it was that some of these able and experienced officers could not be utilised to take charge of such hospitals as Ras-el-Tin, where they could guide the junior staff into the way they should go. It is just another example of not utilising in the right way the wealth of talent which we possess in skilled and able men. I do not for a moment mean to suggest that the talents of these Indian Medical Service officers were wasted on the *Gurkha*. What I do mean is that one or two of the senior men, would have been ample on the ship, with a couple of younger men as assistants, and the other senior men could then have been released for similar work among some of the ill-staffed hospitals in Egypt or Mesopotamia.

Colonel Haig, I. M. S., the senior medical officer on board, was untiring in his care of the sick and wounded, and if a testimonial of his zeal were wanted, it could be found in the difference in the appearance which his three hundred patients presented from the day when they came on board the Gurkha at Alexandria to the day when they left his hands at Southampton. I, who saw it, can only say it was simply marvellous.

After eleven days' treatment in the capable hands of Major Houston, I. M. S., I found myself a different man when I walked off the ship at Southampton, where we arrived on Boxing Day, 1915, and reached London on a hospital train the same evening. At Waterloo we were met by a medical officer, who scattered us throughout the hospitals in London. I was fortunate in being sent to that organised by Lady Violet Brassey at 40, Upper Grosvenor Street, where I was never so comfortable, or so well cared for in the whole course of my life, and for which I tender her my very sincere thanks; and I would also like to thank Doctor A. B. Howitt, Miss Spencer (the matron), and the sisters and nurses for the care and kindness which they showed me during the three weeks I was in their charge.

It was delightful to have old friends crowding in with gifts of flowers, and fruit, and books, and all the latest London papers and gossip. Lady Violet arranged some delightful concerts for us at which such public favourites as Madame Bertha Moore, Miss Evie Greene and others charmed us with song, story, and recitation. Among the "others" was Miss Marjorie Moore, whose song, "Just a Little Bit of Heaven," reached all the Irish hearts there.

Harry Irving, too, came to see me one day, and presented me with a box for the Savoy, where half a dozen of us thoroughly enjoyed *The Case of Lady Camber.*

Discussing the play at dinner in the hospital afterwards, I remarked how well Holman Clarke had acted in the Sherry scene, when the V. A. D. nurse who was at that moment handing me some soup remarked: "I am glad you liked him, because he is my brother."

How wonderfully well the women of the Empire have shown up during the war! They have come forward in their thousands, not only for V. A. D. work, where their help is invaluable, but also for munition work and work of every kind, which up to the outbreak of war it was thought could only be done by men.

Yes, the women have certainly come into their own, and I for one am very glad of it, and proud too of the fact that they have responded so nobly to the call.

CHAPTER XXXI. THE EVACUATION

When I learned in August of the Great Failure at Suvla, and heard with astonishment and no little anger that no further troops were to be sent to Gallipoli, I knew then that the only thing to do was to get out as quickly as possible before the Turks could get a fresh stock of munitions and reinforcements from Germany and Bulgaria.

It must not be imagined that I was anxious that we should leave Gallipoli after all our great sacrifices there, but since the Government had decided once more to fritter away our chances by diverting troops to Salonika, when it was already too late to accomplish any useful purpose there, I knew that our position on the Peninsula was hopeless.

Bad weather was coming on and it would have been absolutely impossible to live in the trenches and dug-outs. Even with the little amount of rain that I had experienced, the communication and other trenches were at times waist deep in raging torrents, carrying down empty cases, dead Turks and other débris.

Had troops been left in Gallipoli for the winter, the losses from sickness and exposure alone would have been enormous; in fact, the Army would have needed renewing every month.

It must be remembered that the conditions of life in Gallipoli were entirely different to those prevailing in France. There were no such things as dry sleeping places, dry clothes, or housing of any kind, and one was just as likely to be killed in the so-called rest trenches as in those on the front line.

One of the saddest things I know of was the death of the Colonel commanding the King's Own Scottish Borderers. He had escaped everything right through the campaign, but in the end met his death in one of the rest trenches about the middle of November, by a shell fired from "Helen of Troy" on the Asiatic coast.

When once it was definitely decided to send no further reinforcements to Gallipoli, of course the only thing left to do was to get out, and to get out as speedily as possible.

But even after the obvious had become inevitable, we still went on gaily, spending enormous sums of money, laying down miles of tramways, making roads, bridges, erecting camp hospitals, and doing a thousand other things—all very expensive work.

When I saw this going on I began to think that perhaps, after all, the Government were really going to do the right thing, which would have been to throw an overwhelming force of Anglo-French troops on the Turks, catching them, as they then were, with but little ammunition, crumpling them up and thus accomplishing our main object in the Near East. This would, undoubtedly, have been the right line of policy to have taken, and would have helped Serbia much more than anything else, but some fatal demon seems to dog the footsteps of our politico-strategists.

When our Foreign Minister declared that we were going to uphold Serbia with all our might he must have known that he was mouthing mere empty phrases, but the unfortunate Serbians put their trust in the pledged word of a British Minister, with the result that thousands upon thousands of them have been cruelly done to death.

The more honest and more noble plan would have been to have admitted that, at the moment, we could do nothing for Serbia or the Serbians, and to have advised them to make what terms they could with their powerful neighbour, assuring them that, at the right time, when we were ready, we would, without fail, not only deliver them from the hands of their enemies, but amply compensate them for the trials they would, for a space, have to endure.

It is said that the gods strike with blindness those whom they are about to destroy and it certainly looks as if the gods had held the searing iron rather close to our eyes; but, notwithstanding all the mistakes and in spite of our politicians and our blundering strategists, and in spite of our neglect of science and scientists, I have still absolute confidence, owing to what I have seen of the splendid pluck and endurance of our men, both in the Fleet and in the Army, that we will come out of this great World War triumphant.

Let it not be supposed that our terrible losses and disastrous failure in the Dardanelles have been altogether fruitless. By our presence there, we held up and almost destroyed a magnificent Turkish Army and by doing this we gave invaluable aid to our Russian ally.

Had it been possible for the Turkish Army, which we held fast in Gallipoli, to have taken part in Enver Pasha's great push in the Caucasus, there is no doubt that the Turks would have crushed the Russians in those regions and have made things look very black indeed for our ally. As it is, I consider it is greatly due to the Gallipoli campaign that Russia, during her time of stress and shortage of munitions, was able to hold her own in the Caucasus and, when she was ready, assume the offensive, resulting in her recent brilliant capture of that great Turkish stronghold in Asia Minor, Erzeroum.

The knowledge that this effort of ours has, after all, borne some fruit tends to assuage our grief for the loss of those dear friends and good comrades who now lie buried by those purple Ægean shores.

We can well imagine that the spirits of those heroes of France and Britain and Greater Britain who have fallen in the fight are eagerly watching and waiting for the hour of our victory; and when our Fleet sails triumphantly through the Dardanelles, as it surely must, and thunders forth a salute over the mortal remains of our mighty dead, their shades will be at peace, for they will then know that, after all, they have not died in vain.

APPENDIX

I had no idea when I was taken to hospital that I should not see my Zion men again. I thought I should be fit for duty in the course of a few days, so I never even said good-bye to them before I left. However, I am in touch with them still through the post, and I am glad to say that there were no deaths after I left and all got safely back to Egypt when that brilliant piece of work—the evacuation of Gallipoli—took place. I promised to recommend those who did well to the Russian Authorities, and I was glad to forward the following letter and list of names to the Imperial Russian Consul at Alexandria, for transmission to the proper quarter:

Headquarters, Zion Mule Corps,
14 Rue Sesostris, Alexandria,
December 14th, 1915.

From the Officer Commanding Zion Mule Corps.
To The Imperial Russian Consul, Alexandria.
SIR,

I have the honour to state that with the approval of your Government a number of Jewish refugees from Palestine, Russian subjects, were formed into a corps for service with the British Army. I have already furnished you with a nominal roll of all officers and men of Russian nationality in the Corps. I now wish to bring to your notice, for the favourable consideration of your Government, the names of those soldiers who did especially well while serving under my command in Gallipoli, and I sincerely trust that you may find it possible to have their names brought before the Imperial Russian Minister for War for favourable consideration.

The following have distinguished themselves before the enemy:

OFFICERS:

1. Captain J. Trumpledor has proved himself a most gallant soldier and has been already decorated by H. I. M. the Tsar for gallantry at Port Arthur.

2. Second Lieutenant Alexander Gorodisky. This was one of my
best officers and he was a very brave soldier. I was much
grieved when he died as the result of the hardships of the
campaign. He leaves a widowed mother who was dependent on him
for her maintenance.

3. Second Lieutenant Zolman Zlotnic, a useful officer and a gallant man.

NON-COMMISSIONED OFFICERS:

1. Sergeant-Major Joseph Yassinsky.
2. Sergeant Nissel Rosenberg.
3. Corporal M. Groushkousky. This Corporal has been awarded
   the Distinguished Conduct Medal for gallantry in the field.
4. Corporal Nehmia Yehoudis.
5. Corporal Isaac Yorish.
6. Corporal Frank Abram (killed in action, leaving a widow and five
   little children).

I have only mentioned those who have specially distinguished
themselves, many others did very good service also, and I am
glad to be able to attach a copy of an official letter, enclosed
herewith, testifying to the good work done by these Russian
subjects while serving under me in the British Army.

Trusting for the favour of your transmitting these names to the proper
quarter.

I remain,
Sir,
Your most obedient servant,
(Signed) J. H. PATTERSON.
Lieutenant-Colonel Commanding Zion Mule Corps.

[COPY.]

8th Army Corps, H. Q. D. Adjt.-General, G. H. Q.

No. 274/12.   No. B. 3322,
October 2nd, 1915.   5/10/15.
M. E. F.
The A. Q. M. G. 8th Army Corps.

I have had a petition from forty-five N. C. O.'s and men of
this corps for permission to go to Alexandria for a couple of
weeks on leave. I would very strongly recommend that this leave
may be granted, as these N. C. O.'s and men have been here (and
have worked well) ever since the original landing in April.

I consider that the men really need this change and as their
families are in Alexandria, I hope they will be sent there in
accordance with their request.

If, as I hope, my men are given leave to proceed to Alexandria,
I propose to give one half leave as soon as granted, and the
other half on the return of the first party.

As these men have done particularly well, I trust that their good
service will be recognised.

J. H. PATTERSON,
Lieutenant-Colonel, Commanding.
2/10/15.
(Zion Mule Corps)

2. Adjutant-General, G. H. Q. 8th Corps, H. Q.
No. B. 332.   No. A. 274/12.
5/10/15   4/10/15
M. E. F.
G. H. Q.

I recommend this application. As the G. O. C.-in-C. is aware
this Corps has done excellent work.

(Signed) FRANCIS DAVIES,

Lieutenant General,
4/10/15. Commanding 8th Corps.

3. *G. O. C. 8th Corps.*
This leave is approved, the delay is greatly regretted, but has been unavoidable. The C.-in-C. has approved of a grant of one pound to each of these forty-five men *in consideration of the good work of the Corps*, and the Field Cashier is authorised to issue the cash.

(Signed) A. CAVENDISH,
Colonel,
5/11/15. A. A. G., G. H. Q.

4. *Field Cashier.*
Please note, and pass to O. C. Zion Mule Corps, who should return this memo to Corps Headquarters.

(Signed) C. D. HAMILTON MOORE,
Lieutenant-Colonel for B. G., D. A.
and Q. M. G. 8th Army Corps.
7/10/15.

THE END

HATIKVOH (THE SONG OF HOPE)

Kol owd Hallivor peneemoh
Nafesch Yehoodée howmeeoh
Uléfahahsi Mizroch kohdeemoh
Aynec Tzeeown tsowfeeoh.

Owd lou ovdoh Sikvohsinu
Hatikvoh hahnowshohno.
Loshur léaretz ahvousinu
Léear bow Dovid chonoh.

Kol owd démohows—Mieyeninu
Yizzlu kéghashem nédovous
Urvovous mibni Amminu
Owd howlcheem al kivri ovous.

Owd lou ovdoh Sikvohsinu
Hatikvoh hahnowshohno.
Loshur léaretz ahvousinu
Léear bow Dovid chonoh.

HATIKVOH (THE SONG OF HOPE)

Arranged by Eva Lonsdale.

By kind permission of Messrs. R. Mazin & Co., London.

1.

O, Zi - on, our fair dwell-ing, home of peace and rest,
Far from thee we mourn our lib - er - ty,
Tho' sadden'd be our hearts, our souls with grief oppress'd,
Still our hope, our hope is in thee.

2.

Tho' dark and drear, the hours pass slow, and fraught with pain,
Still we trust, Thoul't cher - ish us once more
For soon the dawn must break o'er thy green hills a-gain,
Bring-ing joy to thy fair shore.

REFRAIN.

Oh, Lord our God, guard and set us free—
Grant to Zi-on joy and lib-er-ty,
Night and day we pray to be
Once more, dear land, re - stor - ed to thee.

Lightning Source UK Ltd.
Milton Keynes UK
UKHW012025161220
375297UK00001B/92